ANN WATT

Author of *When Being A Nurse Was Fun:*
Tales From My Life as a Nurse

BELIEVE IN
GOD,
NOT COINCIDENCE

Visit our website at **www.StillwaterPress.com** for more information.

First Stillwater River Publications Edition

ISBN: 978-1-963296-52-5

Library of Congress Control Number: 2024910400

Names: Watt, Ann, 1967- author.
Title: Believe in God, not coincidence / Ann Watt.
Description: First Stillwater River Publications edition. | West Warwick,
    RI, USA : Stillwater River Publications, [2024]
Identifiers: ISBN: 978-1-963296-52-5 (paperback) | LCCN: 2024910400
Subjects: LCSH: Watt, Ann, 1967- | God (Christianity)—Goodness—
    Anecdotes. | Fortune—Religious aspects—Christianity—Anecdotes. |
    Faith—Anecdotes. | Trust in God—Anecdotes. | Prayer—Anecdotes.
    | Miracles—Anecdotes. | Inspiration—Anecdotes. | LCGFT:
    Autobiographies. | Anecdotes.
Classification: LCC: BT137 .W38 2024 | DDC: 231.8—dc23

1 2 3 4 5 6 7 8 9 10

Written by Ann Watt.
Published by Stillwater River Publications, West Warwick, RI, USA.

To Christians throughout the world
May we live in harmony with each other

CONTENTS

FOREWORD

MIRACLES HAPPEN IN OUR LIVES EACH DAY. Unfortunately, most of us don't recognize that fact; we think of miracles as huge or noteworthy events. It is a miracle when a child survives after nearly drowning or a fall from a great height. A parent who was mysteriously cured of cancer experienced a miracle. How about when we received a promotion we didn't deserve? Winning the lottery is a miracle.

Does anyone contemplate the miracles which aren't as obvious? Think about the time when you couldn't find your car keys and that delay prevented you from being involved in a multicar accident on the highway. Consider the stranger you spoke with in the supermarket—was it remarkable that they said something you needed to hear that day? Was it a coincidence that you searched a website you didn't normally view, you found something you desired, and it was on sale for half price?

Miracles are custom tailored by God to fit our needs, and He is generous with them. He fulfills desires about which we don't even pray. They may not be presented as big or showy gifts, but in His own timing He provides what we require. I refer to many of the situations in this book as miracles. My personal miracles are mini when compared to world events, but I don't consider them as minor. They impacted my life and were important to me; they reinforced my belief and trust in God. My desire is that these stories will increase your faith as well.

The title states to believe in God, but I also mention Jesus in my memoir. This is a Christian book, and the reader will note that I pray to both of them. God is the Father, and I view Jesus as my Savior and an intercessor for prayers. I wanted to keep the title of this book short—it was not meant to be deceptive.

One of the joys of writing this memoir was that it allowed me to relive precious experiences. As I wrote and edited the chapters, I was immersed in memories of magnificent places, people, and events. I am thankful that I have the opportunity to share these inspirational stories with others.

I hope this book causes my audience to pause for a few moments after they read a chapter. Please take some time and ponder situations which have transpired in your life; something you may have taken for granted in the past may be viewed in a new light. Sometimes blessings are disguised, and you don't realize their importance until they're examined in hindsight. Everything happens for a reason, but it's not because of chance.

RUN OVER BY A BED

NO! THIS CAN'T BE HAPPENING TO ME. NOT NOW.
Why now? Is my ankle broken? Why couldn't they have
sent me home? What am I going to do now? Am I going
to be able to walk on that leg?

Tears started pouring down my cheeks from the
pain that surged through my ankle. I hopped away
from the patient's bed on one foot, not daring to place
any weight on the injured leg. *What a nightmare.* I
was hurt but all the supervisor could say was, "Oh,
you're wearing open-back clogs." Such footwear was
considered unsafe, and employees were not allowed
to wear them in the hospital where I worked. She was
concerned about workman's compensation issues and
not the nurse who was injured in an unusual accident. I

wore that type of clog because they were comfortable, and I never had any problems while wearing them. If I could have turned the clock back by an hour, I would have done so.

My night shift at work started the way it often did: admitting a surgical patient from the operating room. Taking care of a patient who just had open heart bypass surgery meant that I would be busy all night; time would fly by rapidly. That was a good thing during this particular shift, because in less than thirty-six hours, I was going away on a long-awaited vacation. I first had to complete a twelve-hour shift, then I would leave for the Southwest the following morning.

That night demonstrated why the area where I worked was regarded as intensive care. My patient's condition was critical, and his prognosis was grim. What the surgeon noted in the operating room prompted him to have a long talk with the patient's family. They were forewarned that it did not look as though their loved one would survive the night. Despite the staff's best efforts, phenomenal teamwork, and multiple attempts at resuscitative measures, the patient died. It was a grueling night, and his life ended ten hours after the start of my shift.

I silently prayed for him as well as for myself. I was exhausted and hoped that after the completion of the necessary paperwork and physical care, I would be allowed to go home. He had been my only patient; the supervisor might have a bit of mercy on me. Spending that amount of time on your feet is fatiguing, especially in one room with a person who is so ill. The intellectual pressure of making sure everything is being done appropriately, and the emotional stress of seeing a distraught family is often worse than the physical demands on your body.

It wasn't the norm to send a nurse home after their patient died; they remained on their unit and assisted their colleagues. They might have to admit a patient from the emergency department, but I worked in a surgical specialty area. We received scheduled admissions from the operating room later in the day; no patient would be arriving in this unit during the final hour of the night shift. I could have gone home without pay or used an hour's worth of personal time.

The supervisor decided to send me to another critical care area to help out for the remainder of my shift. What I thought saved me was an overhead page triggering a rapid response alert. These notifications were initiated for patients who needed extra attention for urgently developing situations; a patient was deteriorating and needed prompt expertise from a doctor, respiratory therapist, and critical care nurse. This duty was rotated among and assigned to employees from those departments each shift. The team of professionals quickly intervened to prevent a patient's condition from becoming worse. I no longer had a patient, so I volunteered to go instead of the nurse assigned to help during that type of emergency on the general medical ward.

The rapid response patient had developed sudden neurologic changes, and it was determined she would need a CT scan of her head. The primary nurse for this woman had several other patients who also needed her attention, so I was designated to assist with the trip to the radiology department. I didn't anticipate any problems while bringing the patient to that area, but one happened without warning.

While moving the patient's bed through the hallway toward the service elevator, I decreased my pace and pushed a stray wheelchair out of the way. The problem occurred when I slowed down, but the rolling bed behind me did not. I had been pulling the bed by its footboard; another nurse was at the head of the bed, pushing it. Somehow, my ankle became tangled with the large brake pedal on the lower front end of the bed, and my foot was dragged in an awkward motion. The pain was instantaneous. Someone noticed what was happening and stopped the bed, but the damage was already done; my ankle immediately started swelling. I hobbled back to the cardiac unit since I was relieved of CT transport duty. I sat there with a bag of ice on my ankle until the end of my shift; even after my injury the supervisor didn't suggest that I should go home. I should have demanded that I needed to leave, but I didn't; I wasn't thinking clearly due to fatigue, pain, and anger.

I wanted to be examined by an MD and obtain X-rays of the injured ankle. I needed to know the extent of the damage. After the shift was over, I went to the emergency room in the hospital where I was employed. I was told there would be an excruciatingly long wait time before I was examined. No professional courtesies were extended to me regardless of the fact that I was an employee and my injury occurred while on duty. I drove to a walk-in clinic not far from where I lived. I still had to wait, but at least I was closer to my house and not in the city. It was almost one o'clock p.m. by the time I got home, and a short while after that, I crawled into bed. I had been awake for twenty-one hours. The time I got to bed was the hour I had planned to wake up to finish packing for my trip. I managed to obtain a couple hours of sleep, packed the best I could, and then went back to bed again. It was necessary for me to wake up early the next morning in order to catch a six o'clock a.m. flight, and I wanted to be coherent at that hour.

The reality of my trip hit me when I was sitting on an airline seat flying to the Palm Springs Airport. Gazing out of the window, I wanted to put cares about my job, the future, and what had happened the previous morning behind me. The throbbing in my ankle was undeniable, but I didn't have to let the injury ruin the vacation or control my attitude. Thankfully, the ankle was sprained and not broken. I didn't need crutches. I packed a pair of hiking boots, hopeful that the swelling would recede and I might be able to hike short distances. What was the worst-case scenario? I might have to spend the week lounging by the pool while reading a book or sipping a cocktail. Even if I couldn't hike, I would be somewhere other than work or home. I was traveling to a relaxing environment which had abundant sunshine.

Hiking was a hobby of mine and was a factor I considered while making vacation plans. I prefer to visit areas known for their mountains, deserts, or bodies of water. It didn't matter as long as I could spend time outside in solitude. I enjoy immersing myself in nature and exploring it on foot. The region surrounding the Coachella Valley in southern California, where I was going to visit, was full of trails. I intended to enjoy the vacation regardless of whether or not I could hike, but I wanted to explore the desert and mountainous terrain in that manner.

Remarkably, I was able to hike more than I expected. I ace-wrapped my ankle each morning and fitted my hiking boot over it. My vacation was not ruined by the sprain. Hikes that week varied in length and included both sandy and rocky soil. Perhaps I should have treated my ankle more gingerly, but it felt okay. The boot and its tightly wrapped laces provided incredible stability for the ankle; pain and swelling were kept to a minimum.

My foot felt worse when I took the boot off, but during the remainder of the day, it was elevated on a chaise lounge by the pool. Every day I waited for someone to comment on the gruesome combination of colors the ankle was displaying. No one said anything about it or asked what had happened to it either. If they had questioned me about it, I would have smirked and responded, "I was run over by a bed." That would have been a unique conversation starter.

I was satisfied with the way the vacation was progressing and was fond of where I was lodging. I was renting a condo my husband Wayne and I had discovered years ago. The resort consisted of privately owned condos, a few of which were local residents' homes. Several of the units were owned as investments and were utilized for rental income. Others were second homes and future retirement lodging. It was a comfortable and quiet retreat, and being familiar with it made traveling alone easy for me. Wayne was concerned about the small business he purchased in 2009 and made the decision not to accompany me on this trip. I didn't mind solo travel because I followed my own itinerary and didn't have to please anyone except myself.

A couple of faces at the resort were familiar to me. Near the end of this particular vacation, I spotted a gentleman named Smitty. In the past, I was introduced to him during a springtime trip. He was in his sixties and full of life and humor. Making small talk with him was effortless because we didn't focus on any topic for very long. He didn't need encouragement to speak either, since he had an opinion on everything. It was both comforting and entertaining listening to him speak in his European accent. He made me smile and was one of the few people with whom I chatted while I was there.

Smitty joined me in the pool that afternoon after he recognized me, and we started with an exchange of general pleasantries. Our conversation became varied and interesting. It ran the gamut of engineering, electrical parts, border towns, and local clientele. *Wow, can he talk!* He did most of the talking while I listened. I interjected an occasional comment and didn't mind that he monopolized the discussion. I hadn't spoken much with anyone for days and appreciated his good nature and wit.

At one point I realized that we had been lingering in the pool for quite a length of time. My fingertips were beginning to resemble puckered prunes. The sun was inching back toward the horizon and was going to retreat behind the mountains in another hour or so. That was my favorite time of day at the pool, and I wanted to relax in solitude with a glass of wine before sunset. I showed Smitty my shriveled digits and used it as an excuse to vacate the area and retrieve my chilled wine. He understood my hint and said farewell. In an instant, he was out of the pool and departed the area.

As I waded toward the shallow end of the pool, I took note of a different gentleman who had slipped into the water while Smitty and I were speaking. He was leaning against the edge of the pool in what reminded me of a GQ magazine pose. I sensed he was observing me from behind his sunglasses as I made my way past him.

He commented, "Smitty's full of hot air. He just likes to hear himself talk."

His remark caught me off guard, but I responded, "Who cares? At least he's friendly. He's one of the few people who will actually talk to me around here."

"He is so full of bull....I know because I live here. I felt bad for you listening to all that stuff; you looked like you needed to be rescued."

"He's harmless. At least he's friendly. That's more than I can say about a lot of people at the resort. No one else wants to talk to me, so why do you care?"

I didn't give him another chance to reply and was thankful to be out of the pool. I stepped into my sandals, grabbed my room key, and made a hasty exit. While in my condo, I shook my head in disbelief at the brief encounter with the man I had just left in the pool. What business was it of his with whom I spoke? Maybe he didn't like Smitty for some reason, but the old gent was cordial during our encounters in the past. Yes, Smitty was verbose and full of tales, but he put me at ease in an area full of strangers.

What a cocky attitude. That man infuriated me and I instantly disliked him. The stranger didn't bother to introduce himself to me and was full of less than favorable comments about someone else. I started ruminating about our brief exchange of words and didn't want to return to the pool. My vacation, though, was drawing to a close and would be over after another day.

At the same time, I was disgusted with myself for giving the interaction further consideration. He was a stranger and meant nothing to me. Not going back to the pool because of him was idiotic. Even if I decided to have a beverage in the privacy of my patio, I would still have to return to the chaise lounge to retrieve my book and towel. *No one is going to keep me away from that pool. I'll go back and ignore that guy.*

I popped the cork on the wine bottle, filled a goblet, and sauntered back to my seat by the pool. I was not going to forfeit a serene evening in that location. After setting down the glass, I made myself comfortable and picked up my book. The stranger had returned back to his own seat at the opposite end of the water. I sipped and read, oblivious to his movements as if he was invisible to me.

I remember it as though it happened yesterday...

When I looked up from my book, I realized the stranger had slipped back into the pool. He was sitting on the steps of the shallow end near my feet. He was speaking to me again and apologizing for not introducing himself earlier as Alex. As he attempted to make conversation with me, I found him less abrasive than before I had returned to my room. The second encounter was a considerable improvement over the first one. We had a few things in common: careers in critical care medicine, our love of the Southwest, and certain foods. He excused himself and left the area after our discussion ended.

I was now alone at the pool. I admired the mesmerizing view of the sun setting behind the San Jacinto mountain range. I was lost in my thoughts, reliving the events of the day. The sound of footsteps behind me startled me back to the present moment; Alex was walking toward me. He got straight to the point and asked me to dinner the following night. The look of shock on my face must have been obvious, and I hesitated for a second.

"I don't know if you heard me when I was speaking with another couple earlier, but I am married."

"Yes, I heard you say that you are married, but I still want to take you to dinner. I promise to be a perfect gentleman." He handed me a business card and asked me to consider his offer. "I hope you agree to a relaxing meal in town with me tomorrow."

Alex departed again as I placed his card in my book and used it as a bookmark. It was an unexpected interaction, and I wondered how my initial encounter with him evolved into being asked to dinner. I had neither agreed nor disagreed to anything. A decision didn't have to be made until the following day, my last full day of vacation in that locale. In the meantime, the sun was still setting, and I resumed sipping my wine in silence.

On my final day of vacation, I went hiking as planned. My bruised ankle, which displayed a multitude of less than enviable colors, did not fail me. I was blessed with another incredible hike under brilliant sunshine. The midweek hike was in a tranquil area on a ridge, but my mind was not at peace with itself. Alex's dinner offer permeated my thoughts and I attempted to figure out whether or not to join him. Common sense would have flatly said "no thank you" without any further attention to the matter. Somewhere between the mountain trail and condo, though, I made the decision to go to dinner with the stranger I had met the day before.

When I returned to the the pool, Alex was nowhere to be found, and I was dismayed by his absence. It was so typical of my life—offers or promises made to me in the past which never came to fruition. All the mental gymnastics regarding the dinner invitation were for naught. I spent the remnant of the afternoon by myself on a foam raft in the tepid water.

Reluctantly, I returned to the condo because I had to make an effort to start packing my luggage. If I was efficient with that task, I would have plenty of time to go back to the pool and view one more remarkable sunset. The last thing I wanted to be doing in the early evening was packing, but there was no avoiding it. I planned on completing it swiftly as possible. At least the condo had huge windows overlooking the gorgeous landscaping. The fuchsia bougainvillea brightened my mood even though I was leaving in the morning.

When I looked up from my suitcase on the bed, shortly after packing dusty boots and sweaty socks, I saw Alex strolling on the sidewalk beside my two-story condo. I had never mentioned to him which unit I was renting, so he was looking forward. He was probably returning to his home. I ran to the balcony and caught his attention when I yelled down to him.

"Hey there! Is that offer for dinner still open?"

He looked up in surprise when he heard my voice and acknowledged that the invitation was still valid. We agreed to meet at the main exit inside the resort in an hour.

I'm not going to labor over the details of dinner or retell verbatim our conversation. None of those things are important. We drove to the downtown area in a sassy little convertible sportscar and enjoyed a meal in a quaint Mexican restaurant. Alex provided me with pleasant companionship during the evening.

What does matter is what happened in the weeks and months after that dinner and why I was dining with a stranger in this resort town instead of with my husband. While on my solo vacations, I always ate alone, and that didn't bother me most of the time. I don't have to make compromises on where or when to eat, and I set my own schedule and pace. I don't have to explain or defend my choices or thoughts. It's freedom that many people never get to experience. Once in a while, I undergo a twinge of envy when I see a couple who are laughing together and delighting in each other's company. Fortunately, those feelings are rare.

Why do I vacation alone, considering I'm married? There are many reasons, but I think the primary one relates to priorities in life. My husband was not willing to spend a week away from his business in order to spend quality time with his wife. Investing in our marriage wasn't as important to him as it was to me. I always felt that creating memories together was vital to a successful marriage, but he didn't totally share that viewpoint with me. It's impossible to change the mind of someone who is determined to think or act in a particular manner. I learned to embrace traveling solo.

Alex was an amiable dinner companion, and he was generous with compliments. He told me that my descriptions of things were enthralling. I was a novelty to him, most likely because of my New England dialect. His attentiveness was flattering, and he made me feel attractive.

As dinner and the evening were coming to a conclusion, he suggested we meet back at the hot tub near the pool. He wanted to converse with me long into the night. I was suspicious that he had more than talking in mind, so I politely declined. Despite his persistence, I continued to refuse. He had been, as promised, a complete gentleman. I didn't want to ruin the night by doing something I'd regret. I also needed to obtain more than a couple hours of rest because I was returning home the following day. A full day of travel was exhausting, and I was unable to ever sleep during a flight. I thanked him for dinner and returned to my condo by myself.

It was with mixed emotions that I concluded a vacation. On one hand, I was melancholy when I departed from a beautiful region. I was never certain when or if I would ever see that area again. I was guaranteed I would face the same issues at home as before I left on vacation. I would be reimmersed into my daily routine and obligations at work. On the other hand, it was reassuring knowing I was retuning to something familiar which provided consistency in life. My routine was one I devised, and I was not rushed to create memories in a span of a week. My home was where I had control, comfort, and privacy, and I was not living out of a suitcase. I missed my own bed, the sight and scents of my house and yard, and the enthusiastic greeting of my dog. I looked forward to vacation, but I anticipated going home.

One thing that was different about this trip was my departure time at the airport. I usually booked the earliest available flight in order to get ideal connections; I didn't want to arrive home at night. During this vacation, I had a late morning departure, which gave me a few extra hours at the resort. I didn't schedule my flight this way; the airline had changed it. It was a pleasant deviation since I didn't have to wake at three o'clock in the morning in order to catch the early bird plane.

Having completed most of my packing the previous afternoon, I only had to shower and put away a few essentials before I left. Packing for the return flight was what I dreaded the most. On my last day of vacation, I wanted to be at the pool instead of cramming things into a suitcase. That unavoidable task was 95 percent completed, and I was confident I wasn't accidentally leaving anything behind. I decided I would go to the pool for an hour and enjoy the sunshine before I checked out of the condo. The pool was tranquil, and I was enticed to remain there longer than I should. Two hours seemed like two minutes, and I dragged myself back to the room. I couldn't prolong the vacation.

On my way back to the condo, on one of the main paths, I ran into Alex. It surprised me a bit, although I didn't know why. I suppose I didn't consider him a morning person, and I didn't think I would see him again after we said our goodbyes the night before. He explained he was taking his garbage to the dumpster since he didn't want it lingering in his home any longer. I was curious if it was just an excuse to take a walk through the resort, hoping he would see me again. He received his wish if that was the case. I thanked him again for dinner and acknowledged it was pleasant meeting him. He told me that likewise, it was a pleasure, and asked when I was coming back. I didn't know for certain and told him that. He asked me to return, but I made no promises. I smiled and waved goodbye. He remained where he was standing as I walked away.

It was relaxing spending a couple extra hours by the poolside, but that calmness soon dissipated. The check-out process only took a few minutes, but I had to stop and buy gasoline; my rental car contract required me to bring the vehicle back with a full fuel tank. There was a nearby gas station which I had used in the past for refueling. Upon arriving there, I was taken aback by the numerous cars which were in line at the pumps. Obtaining fuel took much longer than I had anticipated.

My next challenge came when I arrived at the rental car return area. I encountered another long line. There was only one attendant checking in the vehicles and handling receipts. I was accustomed to self-check vehicle return before my early flights. It enabled me to fill out the paperwork myself and leave the keys and contract in a drop-box. Such was not the case that day. I anxiously waited as the cars ahead of me were scanned and checked for fuel levels.

A sense of despair overcame me when I reached the line for the airline counter inside the airport. It was at a standstill. I didn't know if there were technical issues or just a massive volume of people for this particular day. Regardless, I was at the end of the lengthy line, and time for me to catch my plane was running out. I did *not* want to be late for my flight. It would be the first time I missed a flight, and it was my own fault for not getting a sooner start to the airport. Because I usually left early, I was not prepared for how tremendously busy the Palm Springs Airport became after nine o'clock a.m. I thought I had given myself plenty of time, but apparently, I didn't.

As I was contemplating how long it was going to take to proceed through the line, I heard someone speaking loudly from behind the ticket counter.

An authoritative sounding voice stated, "Anyone going to Chicago O'Hare, please step up to the counter. Chicago O'Hare ticket holders, please come to the front of the line!"

It was an answer to my prayers. I was going to be allowed to bypass the majority of customers and moved toward the front of the crowd. What I heard next diminished the enthusiasm I was feeling. As I excused myself and worked my way to the counter, I observed one ticket agent leaning closer to another.

She said, "They're going to miss their flight. The security line is over forty-five minutes long right now. They're never going to make it."

I wanted to pretend I hadn't heard those words. I didn't want to believe them. My apprehension was escalating, and I began sweating profusely. The airline personnel quickly checked my bag and gave me my boarding tickets. While waiting in the security screening area, I agreed that they were right; the line was at least forty-five minutes long. That would put me on my flight approximately fifteen minutes after it departed.

Heaven, help me.

No one wants to be stuck at an airport or miss a flight. Perhaps I should have been overjoyed. Palm Springs was a superb city. If I had to be stuck anywhere in this country, I probably couldn't have asked for a much better place. I could go back to the resort where I was staying. All I needed was a few necessities so I could hang out by the pool for a couple of days since it was unlikely that I could get my checked luggage back. It might not be so bad after all, but that's what I was afraid of.

The first thought that popped into my head as I stood in the security line was of the business card that was burning a hole in my wallet. I knew, with a great degree of certainty, that if I called Alex and told him I missed my flight, he would be at the airport within an hour to pick me up. He wouldn't have given me his business card if he didn't want me to contact him.

I could jokingly say, "Well, you asked me when I was returning. I bet you didn't think it would be this soon."

We could have a hearty laugh over it, and he would be overjoyed at seeing me again. I doubted I needed to be concerned over whether there were any available rooms at the resort; he would probably insist that I stayed with him. That was the problem.

I needed to get far away from him and this tempting place. He made everything sound idealistic, carefree, and without consequences. It was deception. I would have to face reality when vacation was over and live with the choices I made. I would pay dearly if I indulged in temporary pleasure which he might suggest. That cost was too high for me. I didn't want to lose my marriage or life in New England. It's amazing how you might not properly value something until you contemplate losing it.

I started intensely praying in a manner I'd never prayed before.

God, there appears to be a slim to none chance that I'm going to make it on the plane in time, but I'm asking you to make it happen. I need to be on that plane and depart from here. I am afraid of what will happen if I don't. I don't want to do anything I will regret, but that's a possibility if I stay. God, help me return to where I belong. If anyone can do it, you can.

The line, which was at a dead stop, started progressing. When I made it through the security area, I sprinted like an Olympic athlete toward my airline gate. Boarding had just begun, and within a few minutes I was in my seat on the plane. I fastened my seatbelt, took in a deep breath, and almost cried.

Safe. I made it. Thank you, God. Without your help,

I would still be waiting in line either at the ticket counter or at the security scanner. I'm amazed at how you did those things. You gave me the favor I needed, and I'm on my way home.

God made the clock stand still while the line inched forward. There is no other explanation for why I wasn't left behind.

This memoir begins with three unrelated events which happened within one week: a sprained ankle, a long-awaited vacation, and an encounter with a stranger.

Most people can identify a significant circumstance that impacted their life. It may be something such as a marriage or the birth of their child. An educator may have said something to you which impacted your career choice. Almost anything, regardless of whether it is positive or negative, may alter your life. The week I described was a memorable one, and through God's incredible power, it triggered a turning point in my life. God purposely combined those individual acts to form a strong foundation upon which He could build up my faith.

I called myself a Christian and never believed I was devoid of faith. I didn't consider myself to be desperate for anything, and self-reliance ruled my life. Without realizing it, there was an unrecognized hunger that existed in me. It wasn't a better job or more attentive companionship that I required. I was starving for more of God and Jesus, and God knew when and how to improve my relationship with them.

God had a plan for me, but I was not privy to His intentions. I didn't comprehend why certain situations occurred. I experienced both tribulations and blessings at strategic moments. When I examined them in hindsight, I understood that everything had a purpose. One of my favorite concepts from the Bible is that not all things are good, but God works all things together for our good. The events in this book didn't take place by chance.

E-ICU

WHEN RUMORS OF CHANGE ABOUND AT work, how many of us feel an initial wave of fear? Is it easier to believe things are going to change for the worse or improve for the better? How many of us immediately start looking for a new job just in case?

I was employed at The Miriam Hospital when it merged with Rhode Island Hospital, which was also located in Providence. Concerns and negative feelings permeated the cardiac ICU where I worked; our jobs were in jeopardy because the trauma center had a similar specialty area. Upper management was eliminating duplication of services, and we didn't know which hospital was going to lose its cardiac surgical program.

Sometimes being at work was miserable but not

because our duties were unbearable. It was due to the growing anxiety about job security that was starting to infect all of us. Everyone wanted to know what everyone else was planning to do. Secrecy and suspicion existed between staff members who were usually friends. If a choice job became available, staff privately applied for it and didn't make its availability known to others. They attempted to minimize competition for the position. At other times, I felt coerced to remain part of the group, whether we all stayed where we were or departed and joined the other hospital. I dreaded being asked the question, "What are you going to do?"

I did not know what I was going to do. I started searching for a new job, but decent ones that fit the criteria of what I was looking for were scarce. I worked twelve-hour night shifts, every third weekend, and my specialty was cardiothoracic critical care. I preferred a part-time job that had benefits and paid as much as what I was earning at the time. It didn't seem like a lot to ask, but the perfect job was nowhere to be found. Yes, I know that no job is perfect. I at least hoped to find employment that was not any worse. Despite seeking jobs throughout Rhode Island as well as the two bordering states, my searches came up void. It was distressing to say the least.

I lowered my standards and looked for jobs that I ordinarily wouldn't have considered. I tried to reinvent my career and seek new challenges as long as I was qualified. *Nothing. Nothing, nothing, nothing.* With each passing day, I became more despondent. I guessed that at least thirty qualified critical care nurses, my colleagues, were doing the exact same thing. It was frustrating and heartbreaking.

One day at work, I received the news that confirmed my worst fears: the rumors were true. The cardiothoracic surgical services in which I had worked for many years were going to remain at our sister hospital; The Miriam Hospital's program would be dissolved. It didn't matter what our statistics were, how many lives we saved, our low mortality rates, or customer satisfaction and community respect. It was all about money and efficiency.

I understood that I was going through what thousands of people experience each year in the United States. Whether it is hospitals, factories, or other businesses combining with each other, the outcome is the same. Some people leave, and some people stay. When mergers were made, a lot of employees lost jobs or the familiarity of a particular job. Promotions, demotions, and overall changes occurred. That was what I was facing too.

Up until the time I heard the official news, I felt I maintained a positive attitude. I was a professional who never spoke to my patients or their families about the upcoming changes. It was business as usual for me, and I tried not to let feelings about my uncertain future impede the care I provided people. That was my work face. My behavior at home was a different story.

I recall sitting outside in my yard on an early summer evening. My husband came home from work while I was sobbing. I had been a reliable employee at the hospital for almost twenty years. Working my way up from being a nurse with a couple years of experience to a seasoned specialist, I mentored new employees. I was occasionally placed in charge of the ward at night. Patients' lives were in my hands, and when they couldn't be saved, I grieved with families as their loved ones were dying. I drew blood with proficiency and knew how to motivate patients to move and take deep breaths after surgery. I always hoped I did more good than harm when following a doctor's orders or family's requests.

I cried relentlessly, wondering what I did to deserve all of this, because I was a dependable and qualified employee. I wanted to be a cardiac critical care night shift nurse. But everything familiar to me was about to change. Wayne knew I had looked for new jobs and there wasn't anything available which suited me. Nothing he said could console me. Why was this happening? It was one of my worst nightmares, and there wasn't much I could do except wait and see.

I give up. I'm not going to look for other jobs anymore. I'll stay where I am and wait.

I was becoming desperate for a way out of my job

situation, but I was long past finding my own solution. Learning to accept things the way they were and making the best of the circumstances was difficult. The cardiac staff faced the same questions and dilemmas I faced, so I couldn't feel sorry strictly for myself. I pulled myself together and went to work as usual on my scheduled shifts. My colleagues did the same thing. We functioned this way for weeks that seemed like years. At least we still had jobs and income.

I refused to talk to anyone about the issues we faced since it did no good; it served no purpose and did not improve our situation. Talking about it turned into heated conversations or complaining, and I wanted no part of that. I dealt with things in my own way and suffered alone in silence. Did I pray? I probably prayed in a hopeful manner, but I don't remember; those days were a blur. What was amazing was how God was able to rescue me in those dark days. He pulled me from a pit of desperation and renewed my strength on one fateful night at work.

I was sitting at a nurses' station with a couple of colleagues as we were catching up on our charting. We were enjoying a lull on a weekend; most of the patients appeared to be resting comfortably with their eyes closed. The critical care area's phone rang, and I recognized the number as that of my friend Lena. She worked a second night shift job taking care of a disabled individual, and she sometimes called to chat to help her stay awake while he was sleeping. She knew this was often a quiet time for us as well, so she took a chance that someone would be available to talk with her. One of the nurses beside me answered the phone, and I signaled to her to hand it to me when she was done speaking with Lena. I hadn't worked with Lena in a while and wanted to say hello. Obligingly, the phone was handed to me after several minutes, and I said an enthusiastic greeting. Lena confessed that she had looked at the schedule in advance and knew I was supposed to be working that night, so she was eager to talk with me.

I never could have imagined where our discussion was headed. As she began to speak, I tried to conceal both the shock and glee on my face. The two coworkers with whom I was sitting were giving me odd and inquisitive looks. I needed to remain silent about the nature of the conversation with my friend because it was heading in an unknown direction. I would not be able to answer their questions, and it was none of their business.

Lena surprised me by notifying me of a job for which she thought I was well suited. I could join her the following week for an informal group interview to check it out. She had been asked if she knew of anyone qualified for the job who might be interested, and my name was in the forefront of her mind. The job required critical care skills and specialty certification. There were both day and night positions available, which were twelve-hour shifts. When she told me about the hourly pay rate, I almost fell off my chair. It was a substantial amount compared to what I was making in Providence. There were other characteristics about the job that made it appealing. I wanted to shout "YES!" but restrained my enthusiasm. We confirmed the day and time we would go to investigate the potential job, then I hung up the phone. The curious expressions on my colleagues faces let me know they were suspicious about something.

"Meeting Lena for lunch next week," I stated before they could ask. It was not untrue, but it wasn't the entire truth either.

The position that Lena had mentioned to me was in an electronic intensive care unit. It's known as an e-ICU and is a form of telemedicine. The job was located in a corporate building in Massachusetts, not within a hospital. The caregivers it employed would remotely access patient data and utilize high-definition audio and video equipment. Our job would entail proactively monitoring patient vital signs, heart rhythms, and laboratory values. We would provide real-time support to the nurses who worked at patients' bedsides in the healthcare system's ICUs. A team of three nurses and a critical care physician worked in the e-ICU on the night shift. Medication or tests could be ordered through the e-ICU doctor. Results of tests could be evaluated, and we could also run code blue events. We were going to be a second set of eyes for the nurses, and it was expected that patient outcomes would improve through timely interventions. An e-ICU was a concept that most people had never heard of in the past, including me. The new e-ICU would be the forty-fifth one created in the United States.

Lena and I were relieved that we were both hired for the job, although we both had trepidation about what lay ahead for us. She left it after a few years because she went back to college and earned nurse practitioner credentials; better opportunities existed for her elsewhere. I didn't know how long I would remain in that job, but it ended up being ten years. I planned on working there until God showed me it was time to leave, and He provided me with new options. When one door closes, another one opens.

This story about a unique job opportunity continues to boggle my mind. Even though Lena told me about the job, it was a precious gift from God. He works through people in a variety of ways. They may help us, comfort us, teach us lessons, and so on. She happened to be the safe portal God utilized to assist and convince me to leave The Miriam Hospital and try something new. The two of us had safety in numbers while we faced an untested fresh start. The timing, characteristics, and quality of this new job were incredible. I could not have found something like this for myself. I suppose that was the point—God wanted to take all the credit for Himself. He waited until I gave up and placed my future in His hands. I failed at finding a job for myself even though I searched at length for an acceptable one. God found suitable employment for me without my assistance. The e-ICU job dropped into my lap from the sky and was a blessing from heaven.

Nothing is impossible with God. In His own timing, He took my dependence and desperation and showed me how He could miraculously change my life. When I was tired of struggling through my own efforts, I was presented with the employment opportunity. Maybe God was waiting to see how long it took for me to show reliance on Him and faith that things would be okay.

I didn't receive the most perfect job on the planet. No job is without problems, and this fact held true for my e-ICU employment. While being trained for the job and through the following months and years, I traveled that rocky road at times. There were nights filled with frustration due to technology issues, colleagues, and our clients. Similar to any job I've worked, there were staffing problems, changes in our required duties, and interpersonal issues. Those types of things were not unexpected and, for the most part, were tolerable. I endured the difficult times because I believed the job was from God and He placed me in it for a reason. I wasn't going to quit when it became challenging. There was something I could learn from that environment other than medical or technical knowledge.

In hindsight, I was correct that working in the e-ICU would teach me important lessons. I wasn't coddled or ego stroked while I worked there; I was shown my deficiencies. Since I wasn't surrounded entirely by friends, I became more aware of the choices I made on how to react to someone's behavior. When negative feelings or actions were directed at me, I learned how to seek comfort from God and rely on Him for strength. During some of my dark times while employed in this job, I obtained inspiration for this book. I became closer to God and started studying His ways. God laid out a straight and narrow path that He wanted me to follow, and it was time for me to begin a glorious journey.

STOP

AFTER MY SPRINGTIME VACATION TO THE
Southwest was over, I kept communicating with Alex.
His contact information was on his business card, and
I sent him a follow-up thank you message for dinner.
Alex and I exchanged emails for three months, and I
learned details about his life. Similar to most relationships, I only knew what was revealed to me. Through
the passage of time, I would be able to form a more
accurate picture of him. Until then, I only had access
to what he disclosed about himself.

Alex seemed to be a witty, good-natured person
who didn't let much bother him. He inquired about my
life but wasn't as forthcoming about his own. I regarded
him as a person who protected his privacy, and I figured

that in time he would tell me more about himself. I felt that emails were a safe mode of communication. There were three thousand miles between us, and we didn't know each other's family or friends. It was comforting having someone impartial with whom to talk, and nothing he read from me was going to affect my daily life. He wasn't going to divulge any of my opinions to my colleagues. I never wrote anything which could be used to embarrass me if he posted it on the internet or Facebook. He didn't appear to be the type of person who would do that sort of thing anyhow.

Those emails provided a welcome distraction from what was transpiring in my life. I was going to accept the e-ICU job, but I had to continue functioning at my current place of employment. I was burying the stress and anticipation of future changes, which included starting a new job in September. Meanwhile, I looked forward to daily emails from Alex. They contained neutral topics and amusing banter. In my naivete, I thought communicating with him was harmless.

Alex encouraged me to write to him. He preferred reading stories about my life versus answering questions about himself. We shared a medical background in critical care, so I knew he appreciated my tales about what happened at work. We had a common bond because we both cared for patients. It didn't matter that we lived in different parts of the country. There were situations which doctors and nurses found comical although the general public might find some of the topics disgusting or in poor taste. I don't believe medical personnel are crude individuals. Maybe some of them are, but I don't think that's the majority. Nurses and doctors are employed in a profession where a tremendous amount of empathy is required. A bit of fun is necessary to break up the intensity and pressure of their job.

I shared stories with Alex whenever I thought of something interesting to write. Some of the stories made me laugh, and others reminded me of times I cried. They all had value in one way or another, and he desired to hear more of my tales. Most people I knew were bored when I spoke about my life, but he told me he loved what I wrote and how I described things. I was flattered, and I had a captive audience. What could be better? My only regret was that I did not keep the original versions of the medical situations, which I described in great detail.

I never comprehended how much those emails were drawing him toward me. I discovered that fact when he began making suggestions after I notified him of my plans to revisit southern California. I would have returned there even if I had never met him since I had been vacationing there for years. It was no secret that I adored that area and always had a terrific time. I was fond of the scenery, hiking, food, and weather. There was no reason for me to alter my usual plans.

Alex's idea of a good time didn't coincide with mine.

He started saying things about staying with him instead of renting a condo of my own. Accepting his offer would have saved me hundreds of dollars. I could have used that money to pay for my airline flight. Common sense and morality, though, dictated where I would reside during my vacation week. The money I saved could not be compared with the ultimate cost to my marriage. I enjoyed my independence and did not want to feel as though I owed Alex for free accommodation. I barely knew him and didn't want to put myself into a situation where I had no escape. Thank God for giving me that wisdom.

Alex pressured me about the condo issue; he didn't want to drop the topic.

"You're a stubborn and difficult woman."

"That's why you find me fascinating. You wouldn't be making that offer if you knew me better."

I resisted his suggestions, but he persisted. Besides his offer of lodging, he tempted me with the beauty of the region where he lived. He knew I loved it there and mentioned that I should visit more often than once or twice a year. He asked me why I continued to remain in an area that had foul and unpredictable weather when the Coachella Valley had a hospitable climate. He pointed out that I could find a nursing job anywhere. There was a fine hospital with a cardiac specialty area a few miles from where he resided. He mentioned how I could hike to my heart's content year-round. I would never have to walk on ice or snow again unless it was my choice. His arguments were valid, but he was ignoring key issues in my life.

I decided the moment had arrived—he needed to be reminded that my life existed in Rhode Island. I had a parent with Alzheimer's disease who was alive and needed me to live near her. It was vital that I ensured she was receiving proper care and her bills were paid. I wouldn't be able to see her often if I resided thousands of miles away. The dog I rescued was a joy in my life. It would be terrible if I abandoned her and she needed to be readopted into another family. I accepted a new job and was starting a variation of my career path after months of struggling at work in Providence. Last but not least, I was married. No number of emails was going to erase the fact that I had been committed to the same person for twenty years. Alex chose to ignore those facts, but I wasn't ready to throw away my entire life and its responsibilities on someone who I met through a casual encounter. The emails were fun, but he was asking me to gamble with my life and insinuated that I should take a chance on an uncertain future.

One response to his suggestions came to mind: "In case you have forgotten, there is a piece of paper in the county courthouse which states I'm a married woman."

It was a blunt reminder that was meant to redirect both of us to reality. I wasn't immersed in Bible study at that time. Otherwise, I may have just come out and said that adultery was a sin, and it was mentioned in the Ten Commandments. I enjoyed our friendship, but we had to draw the line somewhere. My marriage was no surprise to him because I made that fact clear on the day we met. He repeatedly ignored that facet of my life as if it didn't exist. Just because we avoided the subject didn't make it less real to me. I never anticipated his reaction and reply to my marriage reminder.

He wrote one sullen statement back to me: "Okay. Fine!"

There was no discussing the matter with him. He didn't back off gently or understand my viewpoint. Anything I wrote to him was greeted by silence. During the next couple of months before my return trip, I received no emails from him. Just like that, he cut me out of his life. I was astounded. I don't know why I cared what he thought or did, but it bothered me.

I was dismayed by the rift in our friendship. I informed him that, despite numerous emails, I couldn't give up my life for someone I knew in person for less than two hours. He had unrealistic expectations and was furious when I shattered his illusion of our future together. We were unable to have a mature conversation that may have provided closure for each of us.

Alex had plans for me, but those were his own schemes and selfish motives; he didn't care who he hurt in the process. God has plans for us too, but His plans are not meant to harm us. Unlike people, God doesn't cast us aside if we don't follow His suggestions. God is always ready to accept us back and wants a relationship with us. People can and will disappoint us, but God won't, and He is trustworthy. I wish I had spent more time listening to God instead of Alex.

The summer months passed, and I hoped for a fresh start with Alex, but time didn't heal our wounded friendship. I wondered why he was still angry with me. I didn't know how to interpret his silence. Was it loathing, apathy, disrespect, or a myriad of other emotions? One day I realized I was going to the wrong source for an explanation. I stated aloud that God had all the answers. I apologized for seeking them from Alex because he was never going to tell me what I wanted or needed to know.

My September vacation in California began. It was planned months ago, and I hadn't felt the need to cancel it. I continued with my solitary plans and doubted I would accidentally run into Alex. He knew my favorite place by one of the pools at the resort. It would be easy for him to avoid me, and I didn't search for him either. I hiked and toured during the day and returned to the resort in the afternoon. On one particular day, I considered where I wanted to relax—should I choose a location in the sun or the shade? I opted for a chaise lounge in a sunny spot, made myself comfortable, and read a novel. Not long after I arrived at the pool, a few of Alex's friends gathered behind me. I knew who they were, but they weren't aware that I used to be an acquaintance of his. In one of my unanswered emails to Alex, I made a point of telling him I would not approach any of his friends. They did not need to become involved in the friction that existed between us.

I was stunned when his friends started gossiping about him. *What should I do?* It was obvious about whom they were speaking, but I felt powerless to stop them. I was unable to leave my seat and walk away because of my curiosity about him. First, I learned that he was not in the area; he went to visit one of his children who lived in a midwestern state. I was disgusted with them as they proceeded to discuss his life. I was also irate with myself for listening to their conversation, but I continued eavesdropping. My thirst for answers was quenched. After dissecting his life, they departed.

I felt it was God who put me in the right place at the correct time. He heard my cries for answers that I was not going to get any other way. All of Alex's silence was for naught because God revealed his secrets. All things come to light one way or another. I learned about Alex's former relationships, including marriages and divorces; the breakups were painful for him. Alex's friends painted a pathetic picture of his romantic relationships, and it enlightened me as to why Alex acted the way he did.

Even though I was glad to have answers to questions regarding Alex, listening to gossip about him was not a wise thing to do. What I did next was even more foolish—I let him know that his friends were talking about him behind his back. He valued his privacy; they had violated and betrayed him. In retrospect, I realized I was being equally cruel and demonstrated lack of restraint.

Better than anyone else, I understood how words could wound a person. I experienced verbal abuse during my childhood from a relative and a neighborhood bully. Physical trauma can be unbearable, but misspoken words can be hurtful as well. Harsh words leave invisible and memorable scars which we may carry for a lifetime. A sarcastic remark, veiled compliment, or outright negative comment has lasting impact. I felt as though Satan had taken control of my mind and typing fingers when I wrote the unkind message to Alex; I was acting like a stranger instead of myself. I didn't want to be a malicious person and asked God for help.

This has got to stop. Please help me stop.

God didn't need any further explanation; He knew exactly what I was talking about. I needed to modify my behavior and exercise self-control. I lit a candle on my breakfast nook table and got down on my knees in front of it. I stared at the flame and attempted to feel God's presence. In a state of desperation and humility, I prayed to God and repented for my actions. My words may or may not have been harming Alex, but I knew they were hurting me. A dramatic change needed to occur in my life. I believed that God would grant my request. A day later, God made it known that He heard me.

When I arrived home from work the next morning, I checked my email, which was part of my routine. Usually, I was greeted by a gamut of solicitations from retailers with sale offers or coupons. I rarely received a composed email from a friend. At best, I would be sent a forwarded message with photos or trite quotations which were meant to be inspirational. Sometimes I was thankful for those group emails because it meant I was included in someone's contact list. Most of the time I deleted them because there was nothing personal or special about them. They reminded me that no one cared enough to type the words, "How are you?".

On this day, I did receive a personal email; it was as personal as an email became. Its passionate message, though, was reminiscent of underlying rage. The email was from Alex. He didn't write to me anymore, so I was surprised to hear from him. What shocked me the most was the subject line: in bold, capital letters he had written *STOP*. I was afraid to read the contents because I guessed what it might say. In as few words as possible, he told me to stop and that he NEVER EVER wanted to receive an email or text from me again. He emphasized that he hoped I would take this message seriously.

I gave Alex's email, as brief as it was, much thought. Yes, I would comply with his request, but I believed that the order was not from him; it originated from God. God agreed with me that enough was enough and reflected my own words back at me when He told me to stop. It was not difficult obeying God's command because He gave me the strength to do it. I was supplied with an abundant amount of self-control. I gained a newfound sense of relief and freedom after I tore Alex's business card into pieces and deleted his contact information from my computer and phone.

God wanted to be first in my life without any competition or distractions. He had plans for me which did not include Alex, but He utilized him for my ultimate benefit. He wanted me to flourish, increase my faith, and be an example to others. Throughout the next few years, God continued demonstrating His perfect timing and power over situations. It enabled me to write about believing in God, not coincidence.

JM

IT NEVER CEASES TO AMAZE ME HOW GOD works through people and arranges events to fall neatly into place however He desires. A simple word or action from another person can influence our own conduct. He has perfect timing and knows the exact moment we may be open to an idea to do something kind for someone else. He also knows when we are desperate enough to accept help from another person even if we don't ask for it.

Shortly before going on my next trip, I would some-times work on some extra projects in the e-ICU on my day off in order to earn a little more money. The duty involved data collecting, which was monotonous and caused some eye strain from staring at a computer, but the work was easy and the additional income was welcome. On the particular night I planned on performing this extra work, Lena would also be there for her scheduled shift. We could chat with each other while we completed our tasks.

Even though I was going on vacation the following week, I wasn't acting excited. Lena sensed that something was wrong in my life. She was a perceptive sort of gal and observed that I didn't appear as happy as I was in the past. I seemed depressed a lot of the time. I suppose she was right. Despite the fact that she was a friend, sometimes I didn't want to confide in her about personal issues. Even friendships need some boundaries, and I've learned that friendships come and go. At times there were people who I thought were my friends, but they turned out to be untrustworthy gossips. I've developed what I call a healthy level of mistrust for most people. Lena had been a friend of mine for years, but I felt that no one needed to know everything about another person. Some things weren't meant to be shared, and I didn't think she'd understand about my former friendship with Alex. I didn't want to receive a lecture or sense I was being judged.

She couldn't see or know with any certainty what was happening in my life, but God did. He knew I was discouraged and sought joy in the wrong places. Others can disappoint us, but God never fails or abandons us. People or jobs don't provide security in life, God does.

When we place our trust where it doesn't belong, we are usually disappointed. He knew I was desperate enough to accept a plan which was better than any I had ever devised for myself.

I sat quietly while performing my work that night and listened to topics which the other employees discussed. I kept my thoughts to myself and mused about my upcoming vacation. At one point in the night Lena walked over to me with a small bag in her hand. She acknowledged that she knew I liked to read during the plane ride to the West Coast, and she wanted to give me a book that she hoped I would enjoy. She told me that she liked this particular author but warned me it was a religious type of book. The author was a woman named Joyce Meyer. She was well known as a preacher and had her own television series. I admitted I had never heard of her until that moment. The book was titled *Living Beyond Your Feelings: Controlling Emotions so They Don't Control You*. I scanned through it and said that books with religious subject matter didn't bother me at all. My friend reiterated that the author frequently uses Bible references in her books. I thanked Lena and told her I looked forward to reading it. I shrugged my shoulders as I examined the front and back covers. It was a Christian self-help book; maybe that was what I needed.

It wasn't until a later time when I realized those last thoughts were correct—it was definitely what I needed.

It was ironic that my friend gave me a Christian book on what would have been my father's ninety-sixth birthday if he was still alive. He couldn't give me anything like that book because he was dead, but I felt like it was a message from the grave. Maybe he wanted to share with me the things he knew and hoped to save me before it was too late.

God found a way to get that faith-based book to me, and that gift helped change the course of my life. The book caused me to think about things differently, and it renewed my Christianity in ways I couldn't imagine. I believe that every person who returns back to the Christian faith or discovers it for the first time is worthy of a celebration; it is a miracle over which we should rejoice.

My friend continued giving me Joyce Meyer books on various occasions. Both Lena and Joyce Meyer deserved much credit because those books affected me in positive ways. It was God, though, who utilized them as wonderful vessels which brought spiritual messages my way. His word and power alone made the changes in me. He accomplishes what He does in our lives, including the how and when, in ways which are mysteries to us.

I was thankful for that book and for the incredible things that were born from that single gift. It occurred at the right time and place and with the right book. It wasn't a coincidence. This was the hand of God touching my life with His plans for me.

SNAKE

MY NEXT VACATION BROUGHT ME SOME-
where other than where Alex lived, although I loved
the Palm Springs area. God placed a desire in my heart
to see different regions, and He began opening new
doors for me. In the future, I would visit various states.
For now, I was vacationing somewhere that felt familiar but was different. I deviated from my usual plans
and decided to visit Borrego Springs, a town that is
more remote and less congested than the Coachella
Valley. Borrego Springs is located within Anza-Borrego
Desert State Park, the largest state park in California.
It has one of the most diverse desert landscapes in
southern California and is home to the endangered
bighorn desert sheep. Borrego Springs is recognized

as an International Dark Sky community because it protects the night sky from light pollution. Stargazing is outstanding in this area and is something everyone should experience at least once.

I planned a springtime trip and anticipated a magnificent wildflower bloom in the desert and time to explore nearby mountains and trails. There were many state and national parks I had always wanted to visit. The time in my life arrived when I asked myself why I wasn't arranging trips to those places. The simplest answer was that I had a personal comfort zone—areas where I vacationed and felt safe, had developed a routine, and surprises were kept to a minimum. I wanted a stress-free week, which was an excellent reason to take a vacation in the first place. A trip to Borrego Springs sounded ideal.

The winter and spring rains were not plentiful in the Southwest that year, and the wildflower bloom—or lack of it—was disappointing. Local residents I met on the trails informed me of how the area during this particular week should have been carpeted with flowers. In the past, I had experienced phenomenal vacations when wildflowers were blooming in the desert as far as the eye could see. I imagined what I was missing.

A gift that we all have the capacity to carry, though, is being content regardless of our circumstances. Things happen that are beyond our control, and we can choose to be miserable or make the best of a situation. Is it any wonder that so many clichés exist regarding this topic? When life gives you lemons, make lemonade. Life happens. Life is a test. Etcetera.

Instead of focusing on the minimal number of wild-flowers in bloom, I appreciated the other things the region had to offer. Trails weren't overcrowded, skies were clear and sunny, and humidity levels were low. I viewed intense midnight blue skies at night, which were saturated with stars. There was nothing more relaxing than sitting in darkness on my hotel room's personal patio with a glass of wine and stargazing after a fulfilling day of hiking.

I don't know if it was the fresh air, hiking, or wine, but I had vivid dreams while in Borrego Springs. One dream in particular left an unmistakable impression on me. It's not unusual for me to remember my dreams, but this one had special symbolic meaning for me.

Of all the dreams I have had in the past, I never recalled dreaming about my father. He died twenty-five years ago. I rarely dreamed about my mother, and when I did, it was never pleasant—I woke up yelling, recovering from a nightmare. I was astonished that they both appeared in my dream that night.

Within that dream, my parents and I were gardening at my home when we noticed a snake slithering across the top of a wooden privacy fence. He stopped moving and basked in the sun, content where he was situated. I kept my distance from him and remarked that he appeared to be a rattlesnake although they were not known to exist in Rhode Island.

My father, who liked to take matters into his own hands, stopped raking and decided he was going to determine what type of serpent had paid us a visit. He took the handle of the rake and prodded at the serpent, which caused it to rattle up in anger.

Dad turned his back to the snake, and with a smug look, he announced to the rest of us, "Yup, that's a rattler alright."

In the spot where my father stood, the reptile retaliated and wrapped itself around his neck in a way that was reminiscent of a boa constrictor. Then the snake viciously bit him. I yelled for someone to call an ambulance and warned Mom to keep her distance. My mother, who often gave but never heeded instruction, failed to step back. I had the impression she was jealous of the attention my father was receiving. She stepped forward and was also bitten, then the snake returned to the fence and disappeared.

I woke up with a gasp.

I'm okay. I'm okay. I stayed away from the snake, and I didn't get hurt. I had common sense and didn't provoke the serpent. I retreated from him when he was angry. He didn't bite me because I was the only one who didn't antagonize him.

Instantly, I had the revelation to stay away from all the metaphorical snakes in my life whenever possible.

That included people who used me, lied to me, or hated me. God was warning me to refrain from contact with these people. Stay away from the snakes in life and you won't get hurt.

Young men have visions, and old men have dreams. The dream was too real for me to deny its meaning. When I was sleeping and my mind was at rest, God sent me this dream. I mulled that dream over and over in my mind and agreed that it was full of solid advice. God miraculously communicated with me in a way I could understand.

ANGELS AND FEATHERS

MINI MIRACLES PRESENTED THEMSELVES TO me in obscure but innocuous ways. When I had a problem and least expected it, an inspirational word would somehow find its way to me. In the form of sermons, Bible quotations, or passages in books, I received messages of encouragement, confirmation, or revelation when I needed them the most. An appropriate verse appeared when I opened my Bible app to the verse of the day section. Joyce Meyer may be preaching about how the truth will set you free. I discovered the best inspirational books to bring with me on vacations as I wandered through the aisles of bookstores. Whether I found the right message or it found me, there was no doubt that the hand of God or His angels were involved.

There was a time when I contemplated a great deal about angels. I was fascinated with the realm of angels although I didn't idolize them. Fortunately, others shared my interest in angels; resources and reading material about that topic were plentiful. There was even a store called Angel Haven, which was located in a quaint shopping village not far from where I lived. I enjoyed shopping in that area for unusual or artsy gifts which I'd otherwise have to search for through the internet. It was relaxing browsing in the stores of that outdoor mall whether I was looking for something specific or not.

Besides the collectibles shop and the store with pet themed paraphernalia, Angel Haven became a customary stop when I strolled through that shopping area. The atmosphere was soothing, and I admired the glittering angel wing jewelry. I learned the name of my patron archangel, which was Metatron. Sometimes I felt as though the retailers were just trying to sell a little piece of heaven and make money for themselves. Usually, I subdued my cynical attitude. Perhaps they were attempting to sell hope and belief in something good and pure. As long as I didn't place faith in angels above my faith in God, I didn't see any harm in frequenting that store.

I didn't hesitate and bought a book by Doreen Virtue regarding miracles of Archangel Michael when I saw it. Michael was a powerful angel mentioned in the Bible, and I envisioned him helping protect us from the forces of evil. Sent by God, we have spiritual allies who assist us. I pictured angels crossing the boundary between heaven and earth as they performed God's tasks. An angel was sent and gave a message to Mary about her future son, Jesus. Angels also administered care and helped strengthen Jesus in the desert after He was tempted by the devil. Archangel Michael was mentioned in the book of Revelation in the Bible.

I completed reading Doreen Virtue's book about Archangel Michael and contemplated the stories it contained, which were supposedly true. There was a particular facet of the book which intrigued me. It suggested that Archangel Michael had a sense of humor. He left signs so we knew he assisted us or was present with us through an incident or issue. An example of this would be learning that someone who helped you happened to be named Michael. In other instances, a white car—symbolic of purity and goodness—may block you from being in a motor vehicle accident. Better yet, an object such as a feather may appear out of nowhere and signify an angel's celestial business card.

Even though I believed in the existence of angels, I knew that miracles didn't originate from them. God is the one who sends blessings our way. Angels work through guidance from God who instructs them to guard or protect us. Angels are not supreme entities. God should receive all the glory when things go well for us or when we are kept safe. We must not make the mistake of thanking angels and leaving God out of the equation. Express gratitude to God first for sending heavenly assistants to us.

It should have come as no surprise to me that when I desired a message from God, He sent me feathers. I don't recall ever requesting a sign that He heard or would fulfill a prayer. I definitely didn't demand one. I felt that was the wrong thing to do even before I learned from the Bible that you should not test God. Asking for proof that He exists or hears you isn't the correct thing to do either.

God knew me well and knew how I should be led toward Him as I continued growing in faith. I'm an avid bird watcher, and I get excited when I spot a variety of bird I've never seen in the past. I've kept an *Audubon Life-List* birding journal for decades and gleefully document the circumstances surrounding a new sighting. My house was built with birds in mind—it contains multiple windows for viewing nature. Trees and shrubs surround my yard. My home wouldn't be complete without at least a couple of backyard bird feeders and bird baths. Birds have delighted me since childhood, and the world would be less lovely without them. I created a home for both myself and feathered friends who were welcome to visit me any time of year.

I never imagined that God would communicate with me via feathers. It was an astounding and personal way to grab my attention and spoke straight to my heart. A neon sign illuminating the words "I'm talking to you" would not have been more effective. Delicate feathers acted as gentle and caring nudges from God. In diverse situations, feathers found their way into my presence, and they demonstrated how God's timing was miraculous. I appreciated them as special messages that conveyed God's love when I needed comfort.

The feathers may have been calling cards from angels, or they may have been from birds He created. In either case, they were a form of soothing whisper that told me everything was under God's control and would work out for the best.

AIRPORT MESA

AN EXCITING PART OF LIFE WHICH MANY OF us enjoy from time to time is planning a vacation getaway. I loved traveling and seeing new things and anticipated going on an annual vacation. Next on my agenda was a trip to breathtaking Sedona, Arizona, a region of the country that I had never visited.

When I arrived in Sedona, I found the landscape stunning—nothing had prepared me for the area's splendor. What I found even more fascinating was the lure of experiencing for myself the legendary vortex energy of the region. A vortex is considered to be a swirling center of energy that is conducive to healing, meditation, and self-exploration. The area seems to be alive with energy, and many people feel inspired, recharged, or uplifted after visiting a vortex. All of Sedona is thought to be a vortex, but there are specific sites where the energy is more intense.

I was curious about the vortex sites because of their worldwide reputation. Much had been written about those areas. Reading about it, though, wasn't the same as experiencing them for yourself. Each person's individual experience varied. Some people sensed absolutely nothing while others had unique emotional or spiritual experiences. No photo could capture the invisible forces either, but the concentrated vortex sites were located at some of the most scenic locations found among the red rock formations. I treasured beautiful places and wanted to witness the views from those locations.

I felt personal conflict while contemplating that stunning Sedona was also well-known as home to New Age believers. Even though I tried to educate myself about what the New Age group believed, I considered myself to be 100 percent Christian. I had no intention of joining any group who embraces metaphysical spiritual beliefs, and nothing was going to change that fact. I firmly believed in God and was convinced that if any type of energy was felt in Sedona, it originated from God.

Were there evil forces at work there as well? Would I feel either of them? What kind of experience was I going to have? Would it be memorable or something I'd laugh about at a later date?

I would probably be able to say, "I found out for myself what all the hype was about—it was nothing special."

My first hike of that vacation was to a vortex site known as Airport Mesa. I chose that particular hike because the vortex was quickly reached, and there was also a four-mile loop hike which was associated with it. I needed to get used to the elevation and orient myself to the region. There would be plenty of time for longer or more strenuous hikes, so I had a couple of easy routes on my agenda that day.

When I arrived at the parking lot designated for Airport Mesa, there were already a few people exploring the area. I decided to hike the trail around the airport first and then take my time and savor the vortex point at the end of the hike. I wasn't impressed by the size of the vortex area itself. I'm not trying to insult the region when I say it looks like a big lump of rounded rock over which you scramble to the top without much effort. A simple and short trail leads to its apex, and rock cairns direct the way to the top of the oversized boulder in case you can't figure it out for yourself.

I completed the Airport Loop Trail and headed for what was considered the concentrated vortex site. I found a side perch on the mesa that was a short distance away from the people who were coming from or going to the top. Tourists were taking photos and others were meditating and admiring the view. Young adults were doing handstands or precariously balancing on one foot near the brink of the rocks; if you slipped and fell from the edge of that area, it would be catastrophic. The spot where I was seated was as secluded as was possible in that popular area—which meant that it was not private at all. My back was turned toward everyone, and I scanned the beauty of the region while I attempted to tune out the distractions.

What immediately came to my mind was a wave of thankfulness to God for getting me safely to this location and for prompting me to make the arrangements to come to Sedona. I was here, in His care, and I wasn't worried that anything bad was going to happen to me during this trip. The grandeur was overwhelming, and it was unfathomable how someone could believe that anyone other than God devised the magnificence that surrounded me. How the rock formations and color combinations were created was inconceivable; it was an area of pure genius. It was thoughts such as those on which I meditated as I sipped my water and admired the views.

Even though I sat on the vortex itself, thoughts of vortex energy were not my main focus. I was not waiting for something to happen so I could run and tell someone about a sensational experience. I existed in the current space and time and remained relaxed. I enjoyed my morning and the surroundings. It was during that state of peacefulness and meditation when I felt the oddest sensation overcome my body. I looked down at my arms, and the fine hairs were standing on end while a tingling sensation made my body shiver. The feeling caught me off guard, and unconsciously, I tried to shake it off. I experienced the cool chill for another few minutes and then it was gone. It was a strange feeling, and I looked around to see where the breeze was coming from. There was no wind, and I was sitting in an area filled with sunlight. I looked at my arms again. Perhaps I had been sweating and the perspiration was in the process of drying. I was perplexed because it wasn't that hot out and my skin wasn't moist.

Without knowing why, I spoke the words and asked, "God, is that you?"

I received no answer.

Soon after, I left the vortex and continued to my next hike, which was not far down the road. The day was young, and I planned to hike to a small hilltop called Sugarloaf Mountain. I planned on hiking until I was just short of exhaustion because there were so many things I wanted to see during that vacation. I desired to complete a variety of hikes that gave me varying views of the region's rock formations. I figured the brief Sugarloaf hike wouldn't be challenging.

I made it to the top of the mountain and was joined by an elderly couple who lived locally. They knew the area well, and they were physically fit from their daily hikes or walks. It was nice to see that even though they lived in the region, they did not take the beauty for granted and continued to enjoy it on a regular basis. We had a pleasant conversation, and they inquired about my travels in Sedona. I admitted I wanted to visit the various vortex sites, but I confirmed that I was a Christian. It seemed as though they were relieved to learn I did not practice New Age ideology. At that point, the woman leaned slightly closer to me.

She whispered, "That's good, because there's a lot of element around here. You know, evil. You can feel it at times; it's infiltrated the area."

I acknowledged, "I believe the spirit of evil exists, but the power of God is greater. I hope that whatever I feel in Sedona comes only from God."

Those words barely crossed my lips before I felt that same strange tingling sensation again. I stared in disbelief at the hairs that stood up straight all along my arms.

She noticed it too and said to me, "You are a true believer."

No further discussion was necessary, and we hiked away from each other in opposite directions.

I knew that what happened that day was a miraculous gift from God even though there was no mention of that sort of thing in the Bible. Why? Because the tingling sensation continues to sporadically happen to me. I cannot say it randomly happens because that would be an incorrect description. It usually occurs when I seek or praise God or when He sends a word of acknowledgement to me. Sometimes I ask for help from God when I don't know what to do. I may be thinking about helping or encouraging another person. It's on occasions like those that I feel that familiar chill and tingle. The first time I felt those things was in Sedona, but nowadays, it doesn't matter where I may be or what else I may be doing; the common denominator is that God is on my mind.

My tingles are a heartwarming type of guidance. I feel blessed because I don't personally know anyone else who says they truly feel like they hear from God. I didn't know why God gave me this gift, but I learned to appreciate not question it. Considering we should believe and not ask for wondrous signs, I am utterly amazed that this wonderful sensation and message of confirmation gets sent to me.

I have learned a valuable lessons from this gift; it is to have greater respect for God and what He is able to do for us. It is His will to bestow favor on us as He chooses. I'm learning to be still and listen for His guidance. When I was tranquil on the vortex rock perch, He presented this phenomenon to me. What the woman on Sugarloaf Mountain witnessed has been revealed to only one other person before this memoir was published; I have not shown or spoken of these shivers and goosebumps to anyone else. I know that eventually someone will ask me to demonstrate it to them in order to prove it.

I cannot shiver on command and make my hairs stand up on my arms because someone demands to see it. It happens during a moment when I communicate with God and feel a special bond with Him. I imagine how insulting it will be when someone says to me, "I don't believe you." Isn't that what many of us do to God on a regular basis? We don't believe in God, and we ask Him for signs to prove He exists. The valuable lesson we need to learn is that God is sovereign and does not need to prove a thing to anyone.

COURTHOUSE
BUTTE LOOP

WHILE VISITING SEDONA, I KNEW I WOULD never be satisfied with enjoying the outstanding red rock views as merely a car tourist. I consider a car tourist to be someone who drives through an area but doesn't take the time to savor or explore it beyond a few feet from their mode of transportation. They might stop at a parking lot or pull-out space along a road just long enough to take a few snapshots or selfie photos, then quickly continue on to another destination. They view the beauty from the comfort of their vehicle but don't immerse themselves in anything that requires more effort than driving. Not everyone is physically able to hike, but I can. I was determined to enjoy the myriad of trails throughout that scenic region. I had tentatively planned a hiking itinerary prior to my arrival in Sedona, and Courthouse Butte Loop was near the top of the list. The loop encompasses Bell Rock and Courthouse Rocks. Bell Rock is well known as another vortex site. I did not have any particular expectations except that I would view the fantastic structures created by God.

Immediately after I started the hike, I began to note increasing cloud formations to the north. The forecast was for a partly cloudy day, so the clouds were not unexpected. I loved hiking under brilliant blue skies, which the Southwest often provided, but I have learned to appreciate clouds from a photographer's perspective. Clouds added depth and more interest to what might otherwise be an ordinary photograph in an extraordinary place.

I initially welcomed the clouds. They made the photos more dramatic, and they kept the crowds away. Anyone who has spent time hiking in the Southwest or desert regions is wary of clouds and the potential rain they may bring. Flash floods may instantaneously appear as the ground fails to absorb rainwater, even if it is raining miles away from where you are located. When a couple of raindrops moistened my skin, I should have known better and returned to the rental car. I wasn't concerned about my own safety; I was worried about keeping my camera dry. The rain stopped after a few moments, and I continued hiking the loop.

I watched the clouds build all around me as I admired the scenery. The recent monsoons had left the area full of wildflowers in bloom at the base of the rocks and along the trail. Digital photography made it easy to capture the beauty, and I became engrossed in taking photos.

At one point, I looked up and was astonished at how fast the clouds had encircled me. It was as if there was a donut ring of clouds overhead, and I was standing in the middle of a sunshine donut hole. But donuts were not what I was thinking about. As I continued hiking, a ray of sunshine followed me wherever I went. I felt as though a pair of invisible angel wings were spread open over me while God's light illuminated my path; I was shielded from rain and harm.

When I arrived back at the rental car, I observed the wet pavement in the parking lot and on the nearby road. I drove toward downtown and noticed that there were numerous dark clouds that had overtaken the entire area. I decided that the best course of action was to return to my lodging at the bed and breakfast inn.

The B&B owners, Mike and Milena, seemed glad I had come back safely. Each morning, I notified them of my tentative hiking plans in case I did not return due to a mishap of some sort. They were surprised I hiked—they were certain I had aborted my main plans although they knew I was determined to take photographs of something one way or another. They described the downpouring rain that had occurred that morning and how it seemed no region was spared—no region except the space above my head as I hiked.

I could say it was dumb luck that I didn't get drenched, but I truly believed an angel sent by God hovered over me, and a pair of celestial wings protected me like an open umbrella. Luck doesn't bring you peace. Imagining and believing in a heavenly guardian is what gives a person an immense amount of peace.

SEDONA
HUMMINGBIRD
GALLERY

BIRDS HAVE ALWAYS BEEN SPECIAL TO ME, AND one of my favorites are hummingbirds. Unfortunately, only the ruby throat migrates to the Northeast and resides there for a few months each year. When I have the opportunity to see a greater variety of birds while on vacation, especially hummingbirds, I am thrilled. An additional bonus while traveling is finding stores that specialize in bird or nature items. I discovered a terrific business called The Hummingbird Gallery when I visited Sedona.

The proprietor of this shop, Beth, was cordial and knowledgeable about birds. Her store was loaded with hummingbird themed items, including jewelry, sculptures, and ornaments. Narrowing down my choices of what to buy was difficult. One item I decided to purchase was a solid sterling silver hummingbird pendant. It was simple yet elegant, and it would be a reminder of my scenic and serene trip to Sedona. Beth told me it was $60, which at the time seemed a small price to pay for a memento of a place and bird which I had grown to love.

My purchases were tallied, and I paid with a credit card. She offered to polish the pendant to give it extra luster and took it into the adjacent room.

Immediately I heard her exclaim, "Ooh! Oh! Oh no!"

Beth returned to the showroom with the charm and notified me that she had undercharged it—the actual price was $120. At that point, she didn't know what to do next.

I had seen the price tag on the underside of the pendant before I bought it, but she quoted a lower price. There was a sale banner hanging over the doorway, so I thought jewelry was included in the sale. It was an honest mistake, and I considered my options on how to proceed: I could tell her that I desired a refund because I did not want that piece for the true price, or I could be a jerk about it and tell her the purchase and payment had already been completed and it was her problem. Before I knew what I was going to say, I pulled out my credit card again and handed it to her. I told her to charge the remaining cost of the item. I notified her that my husband was also a small store owner and I understood how he would have felt if something like this happened to him. Such an innocent mistake eats into profits, and in this economy, every purchase counts.

I walked out of the store and was determined to enjoy my pendant, even if it wasn't the bargain which I originally thought it would be. I decided to be satisfied that I did the right thing, and I wondered if Beth appreciated my actions. What would you have done?

This story may seem pointless if it ends at this moment, but it doesn't. Sometimes our actions have consequences or benefits in the future that we cannot predict.

A couple days after my hummingbird store shopping episode, I was packing my luggage before coming home. I have always been good about keeping my baggage under airline weight restrictions on the way to my destination. Buying bulky or numerous souvenirs, though, made packing for the return trip challenging. I knew my bag was going to be terribly overweight, and it was too late to find another way to ship my purchases home. Packing was completed and I hoped for the best.

When I arrived at the airport check-in counter the next day, my baggage fears were realized. I had prepaid for my luggage, but when it was placed on the scale, I was notified I would incur additional expensive fees. It was estimated my suitcase would cost at least an additional $100. I shrugged my shoulders and took out my credit card. The airline representative worked on the computer and attempted to reprint a baggage tag and charge the fees. I bet by now someone else might have been having a fit of rage, yelling at the representative, making obnoxious comments, or showing impatience at how long the whole procedure was taking.

"It's not your fault I overpacked, I know you're just doing your job. I went a little overboard while shopping. Shipping my purchases home through the mail or a courier service would probably cost an equal amount."

He looked at me and stated, "You're all set."

"Do you need to see my credit card or is the number on file? I prepaid the original fee."

"I'm having a problem with the computer. You're all set."

It took me a few seconds to process what was happening—he was *not* going to charge any additional fees. I wholeheartedly thanked him, wished him a terrific day, and left before the computer started functioning properly or he changed his mind. The last impression I had was of him placing a huge orange *VERY OVER-WEIGHT* sticker on my suitcase.

Does the hummingbird gallery story make sense now? What if I had cheated Beth out of the correct purchase price or was rude to her? I was certain I would have paid an equivalent amount for my luggage. Instead, I was generously given a free pass on a grossly overweight bag; the money I saved paid for the pendant. It gives new meaning to the phrase "you reap what you sow," doesn't it? Was this a coincidence? Definitely not.

BREAKFAST
NOOK TABLE

BY NOVEMBER, I HAD GROWN ACCUSTOMED
to receiving periodic feathers. They were one of the
ways I felt God spoke to or acknowledged me. The
timing of His feathers was remarkable. I found them
stuck in my hair or on the ground at my feet on hiking
trails. I witnessed them floating out of the sky on a
gentle breeze as they landed in my yard or driveway
at home. Once, I spotted one attached to the hind leg
of my dog. They mysteriously appeared when I was
deep in thought about significant issues in my life. If
I was contemplating a problem about which I needed
to make a decision, I would discover a feather when

I gravitated toward an acceptable solution. God let me know when my thoughts or actions were right on course. Finding feathers gave me encouragement and showed me God heard my dilemmas and that He wanted to guide my actions. The feathers brought me comfort in many ways, and I appreciated their beauty and sudden appearance. I came close to depending on them when I needed to hear from God, especially if I had a question and desired an answer.

On a chilly day in November, I started feeling dejected. The devil and his demons have a way of playing with your mind and they plant seeds of doubt. I became discouraged because I was underestimating the power of God, and I felt guilty for relying so heavily on those feathers, which I considered spiritual signs. I didn't ask for signs from God, but I was always thrilled when I received one. I knew it was wrong to test God, but that was what I sometimes felt I was doing when I hoped to see a random feather at a strategic moment.

The devil didn't want me believing in God or messages from heaven; he was determined to destroy my faith in God. He tried convincing me that the feathers I received were nonsense and mere coincidences.

"What do you expect?" he yelled in my head. "You live in the country; you're surrounded by trees; you lure birds to your yard and feed them. Birds lose feathers; they molt, and they get attacked by other birds and cats. Naturally, you're going to find random feathers, especially in your yard."

He was trying to deceive and confuse me, and I was starting to believe his lies. To compound the issue, it was getting colder outside since winter was approaching. I admitted that I usually didn't spend much time outside during those months. *How am I going to find feathers now?*

I was alone in the house, cleaning, and I was on the verge of shouting when I demanded, "Yeah, God, how are you going to send me feathers? I'll be inside during the winter, so I won't see another feather until spring." *Maybe those previous feathers were coincidences. Maybe I wasn't hearing from You after all.*

At that point, I tried to banish the skepticism from my mind. I continued pushing the vacuum around the breakfast nook. I knew dog food kibbles sometimes ended up under the nook table pedestal, but the vacuum brush was too bulky to fit under those legs. I decided to wipe them up by hand. When I knelt to clean the area, I felt the crushing blow of God's superiority, and a reverential awe of God struck me. I spotted a tiny, delicate, pure white downy feather caught in a spider's web under the table. I imagined God laughing and sarcastically asking me if I still doubted Him.

"If you need me, I can find a way to contact you. All you need to do is believe and keep your mind and heart open to me."

Nothing is impossible with God.

THE WORD

WHEN I STARTED TAKING MY WALK WITH God more seriously, I wanted to work on becoming a better Christian. How should I begin my self-improvement task? I thought about something I always wanted to do, which was read the entire Bible. It sounded like a good plan.

There were many things I wanted to accomplish before I died, and I've kept a mental list for decades. Most people called it a bucket list. Some of my ideas were grand or expensive while others were simple. Goals that don't require an enormous amount of time or effort, though, are often on the low end of the priority scale. I wondered why reading the Bible was at the bottom of that list when it should have been at the top.

Selected verses of the Bible were read in church, but that barely scratched the surface of what that book contained. I listened to what was preached but didn't fully understand or apply what was taught. I finally hungered for the Bible because I knew I was missing important lessons. I wanted to say I read through the whole Bible at least once in my life, but I didn't appreciate the difference between reading the Bible and studying it. We all have to start somewhere, and there is a learning curve to any new endeavor. My intentions were sincere, even if the method fell short. I was embarking on an overdue spiritual journey. I found a Bible app on my iPhone, which had free reading plans of various themes or chapters of the Bible. I picked one that gave me scriptures to read every day from beginning to end. I would complete it in a year.

My project had potential, but it fell short even though I accomplished my goal. The problem was that I squeezed in twenty minutes of Bible time before I drove to work or went to bed. Sometimes I listened to it via a narrative feature on the app while I walked on a treadmill. I confess that I fell asleep on the sofa a few times while listening to it. Some days, if you asked me what I had just read or heard, I wouldn't be able to tell you a thing. On a few good days, I highlighted and bookmarked verses that appealed to me, especially if they were relevant to a situation I was going through at the time.

One day, it dawned on me that reading through the Bible was not enough; I needed to study it. Its contents would improve my life but not if I rushed through the verses. If I wanted it to help me strengthen my Christian faith, I needed to delve deeper into the scriptures. It had been foolish to read the Bible in order to place a completed checkmark on my to-do list. God was not impressed with my diligence because I inhaled His nourishment, the bread of life. I devoured it in a year but didn't take time to savor it.

I searched for a Bible that would help me not only read but examine and dissect the Good Book. I learned there were bibles with dictionaries of terms used and explanations of verses within the pages. There were translations of the Bible that I never knew existed. Prices varied, but I was making an investment in myself not an ordinary book. I wanted one which was well-constructed and that would withstand time and use. I was unable to decide which one to purchase, so I waited. My birthday was coming up in a few weeks, and I figured I would buy a Bible as a gift for myself. I had time to research which one I wanted before that special day, and I planned on buying one that would last a lifetime. My birthday was in January, so I had the opportunity to acquire a gift which symbolized a fresh start in both my life and the calendar year. What a beautiful way to celebrate another year of existence.

My friend Lena was the only person who knew I had

tried the Bible in a year reading plan. She also knew I enjoyed reading the verse of the day on the app. Other than that, I didn't speak of Bibles to her or anyone else; she didn't know I planned on purchasing one. I was caught by surprise when I walked in to work one day and found a gift bag with my name on it. Wrapped in tissue paper was a *New International Version Life Application Study Bible* with my name engraved on it with gold lettering. That Bible included maps, a concordance, and its own reading plan suggestions; it was the kind I wanted to purchase. My favorite parts were the verse explanations at the bottom of each page. There were anecdotes and charts with mega-themes of each chapter and in-depth profiles or biographies of important people mentioned within the Bible. It contained a wealth of information and was the most comprehensive Bible I had ever seen.

I thanked her and conveyed that the gift was appreciated. The present appeared to be a remarkable coincidence, but it wasn't. God prompted her to buy it for me, and in doing so, He fulfilled a desire of mine. I think God was pleased that I wanted more of Him in my life. I was trying to diligently seek Him and become a better person. He helped me continue toward my goal with access to as much knowledge and truth as I could consume. God didn't give me birthday cake to fill my stomach. Rather, He gave me something that nourished me spiritually.

My delay in purchasing a Bible for myself wasn't accidental. It was part of a greater plan, and I treasured that Bible for many reasons. The precious and timely gift contained truth and knowledge within its covers. I studied the book of Psalms, which described how to be thankful and praise God. The book of Proverbs taught about wisdom. The Old Testament showed what life was like before the Jews had a savior. The New Testament contained the parables of Jesus and explained how Christians should live. The Bible helped me in other ways: I learned about the Fruit of the Spirit, which is love, joy, peace, patience, kindness, goodness, faithfulness, gentleness, and self-control. The Bible explained why those characteristics are beneficial to us and how we can demonstrate them to others.

I love that Bible even though I don't read and study it as much as I should. It is comforting to know that, like God, it is always available to me when I need it.

MOOO7

I LEARNED FROM PERSONAL EXPERIENCES that making new good habits was easier than breaking detrimental ones. Reading the Bible was a beneficial habit I established in my life. Thinking about Alex was a harmful practice which haunted me from time to time. Our relationship had flourished for a few months, but it ended as quickly as it started. I wanted to push memories of him out of my mind. Inevitably, when I thought I had forgotten about Alex, something would remind me of him. At times, I felt I took one step forward and made advances in my life, and then I took two steps backwards. We all go through that sort of progress and regression at some point in life.

On this particular day, I was on the internet and

looked at news websites. I read about the torrential rains in southern California that resulted in massive street flooding in many areas, including the Coachella Valley. I knew that a few roads close to where Alex resided were notoriously prone to flooding when it rained in the mountains and deserts. It was a headache for both tourists and residents when precipitation overtook the area.

Despite the hardships the deluge caused, it made me giggle a little bit. Alex fancied fine cars and owned a couple of them. I pictured Alex driving out of a huge puddle on a flooded road in a similar manner to a scene from a James Bond movie. In *The Spy Who Loved Me,* Bond's Lotus car sprouted fins and maneuvered out of the ocean. Alex could be a new movie character named Dr. Bond. Even though Alex was a physician, I didn't call him "doctor." He deserved to be addressed by his title, but we were friends and he never requested that I do so.

The weather on the East Coast contrasted what was happening in California; it was mild and free from storms. I put thoughts of Alex behind me and focused on getting to work. The drive on Route 95 diverted my attention to more important matters such as getting to the job safely with my car and life intact. I remained always alert for other drivers and was a firm believer in defensive driving. I kept an eye out for potential trouble. I liked looking at cars and interesting license plates, so the ride to work wasn't terrible all the time. I spotted a foreign high-end car with what I thought was a cool license plate.

"Look at that, how cute."

MOOO7. I didn't think a Mercedes driver would be interested in cows or inclined to put something like that on a license plate. *Maybe he's referring to the cattle drive that's also known as the commute on the highway. That's pretty funny.* When I got closer to that vehicle, I noted the registration didn't say *MOOO*. It was *MD-007*, just like Dr. Bond.

I was like a cat that had the proverbial nine lives. Anytime something strange like that happened to me, I thought my heart stopped beating for a few seconds. What kind of bizarre coincidence was this? There was no rationalizing it in my mind. I never told anyone this story because most people would think I invented an outlandish tale to get their attention.

There is no doubt in my mind that God sees everything. He knows our deepest, unspoken thoughts, and He hears our prayers. God knows if our intentions are good or evil and what is on our minds. This was another example to me that He would not be fooled. God had His finger on the pulse of my life and knew exactly what I was doing all the time. Each incident like this reinforced my attempts to be more obedient to God and careful about what I thought, said, or did.

It was improbable that a car with fins in a movie, Dr. Alex, and that license plate would all be noted within the same day; it was beyond belief. Unless you believe in God.

UA434

MORE THAN WE CARE TO ADMIT, WE HAVE little desires in our heart that we hope become reality. Sometimes wishes do come true—they brighten our day and put a smile on our face. The minor desires that are fulfilled have a way of sustaining us when things around us are going wrong or when we need a pick-me-up during the day. Their timing is incredible, and they bring pleasure well beyond what they are worth. They are things like finding your favorite jeans on sale, and you are able to buy the last pair in your size. How about when you were craving something sweet to eat and a friend baked your favorite cookies for you? It's having perfect weather during a summer party or outdoor event that you are attending. There are many things we don't have control over in life and about which we don't have any foreknowledge. We are overjoyed when circumstances work in our favor. I think it is a way that God blesses us from time to time. We need to appreciate those moments and express gratitude to God.

One of my secret desires is something over which I definitely have no control, but I still wish for it. Whenever I need to take an airline flight, I hope no one will be sitting next to me, especially in a plane that has seats grouped in sets of three. At the very least, I want to be seated next to someone personable. I have been fortunate in this respect on most flights, so I shouldn't complain. Nowadays, most planes are overbooked, so the chances of sitting alone—or nearly alone in a row—are slim to none.

While I was waiting for my flight from Chicago to California to finish boarding, I watched the passengers as they entered the cabin. Each person who walked toward me was a passenger who might be seated next to me. One by one, people continued down the aisle toward the back of the plane. As I scanned the crowd, I wondered who would be sharing the confined row with me. A gentleman took the aisle seat; I was seated next to the window. We exchanged hellos and waited.

A few moments later, we heard a sound which was pleasing to our ears: the airplane cabin door was being closed by a flight attendant. An announcement was made that we would begin taxiing to the runway, and the crew were preparing for takeoff. Simultaneously, the gentleman in the aisle seat and I exchanged glances and huge smiles. We were both thrilled that no one was sitting between us. This meant we each had extra leg room without encroaching on the personal space of someone seated between us. Neither of us was ever that fortunate or had much elbow space in the economy cabin. What made the situation special was the fact that we were on a popular four-hour flight to the West Coast. Gone were the days when I had enough frequent flier miles and was able to upgrade to first-class cabin seating that was less cramped.

I stretched out my legs after I retrieved a book out of my backpack and set myself up for relaxation mode. The additional space was welcome, and the man next to me was cordial. I had no complaints and minded my own business. When the beverage cart started rolling my way, I planned on asking for my usual choice: it was either a cup of orange juice or a diet cola, depending on the time of day. Staying hydrated during the flight was important, and I was going to choose the juice because it was morning. Before the flight attendant had the chance to wheel the cart further down the aisle, my fellow passenger turned to me and asked if I'd like an alcoholic beverage. I must have had a surprised look on my face; no one ever offered to buy me liquor during a flight. I admit that I am too cheap to buy overpriced drinks in a plane even though I would enjoy one. I figured I would consume enough alcohol when I reached my destination. My temporary companion continued by saying he was flying to see his son who was returning from a military tour of duty overseas. He asked me to have a celebratory drink with him because he was grateful his son made it back home unharmed. I appreciated his kindness and sincerity, so I agreed to an alcoholic beverage; we toasted to the military and his son's safe return.

I wanted to demonstrate some thoughtfulness in return. It was a minute gesture on my part, but I shared my favorite smoked almonds which I had brought along as a snack. I was astonished that he never had that type of flavored nuts in the past, and he immensely enjoyed them with his beer. We spoke about trivial things, and he shared some stories that made me chuckle. Without asking, he bought me another drink, and we passed the time with brief conversations which alternated with periods of silence. He occasionally napped while I read my paperback. The flight was smooth and peaceful; its duration felt shorter than four hours. The pleasant hours we spent together were drawing to a close; our fellowship would dissolve when we reached the airport. I am ashamed to say that I never introduced myself. We had talked and laughed; our names didn't matter.

As the flight attendants were clearing the cabin and preparing for the descent to land, my transitory companion took out his credit card to pay for the drinks. He had run a tab instead of being charged for each individual beverage. As his credit card lay on the tray table between us, I was able to glimpse at the name on the card. I didn't see what his last name was, but I noted that his first name was Michael. Should that have come as a surprise to me? I believe God has a great sense of humor and ingenuity.

I had read the book about Archangel Michael the previous year and was amazed at the ways he was used by God. Michael's duties included protecting us and bringing peace to the world. God sent me a Michael in the form of a military veteran, an upstanding man who wanted nothing in return from me. It was a discrete blessing that meant a lot to me at the time. I still fondly remember that flight.

Upon reaching the baggage carousel, I said goodbye to Michael and thanked him again for the cocktails and helping me pass the time. I let him know I appreciated being seated next to him. Without prolonging the inevitable, we parted our separate ways.

I was content with the brief camaraderie we shared during the flight, but I kept that interaction to myself for years. In this day and age, many people are suspicious of the motives of others. Who would believe that drinks and laughs among strangers did not include any hidden agenda or future rendezvous? I knew what transpired that afternoon and the way God blessed me with a serene and delightful flight. God knew my secret desire to have sufficient space next to my seat as well as a pleasant stranger seated in the row with me. The flight was beyond my expectations. God never ceases to amaze me, from something as simple as an airline flight to the larger problems of life.

When we trust God to take care of the miniscule things and see that He is good, we grow in faith and trust Him with major issues. The same goes for us as well; we should strive to do the right thing when small or insignificant issues are involved. God sees when we are trying to make correct choices and behave with integrity. He will entrust us with greater responsibilities and blessings in the future. Be thankful for a patient and generous God whose creativity in every situation knows no boundaries.

MOSES AND
MCGURK MEADOWS

I HAD ANOTHER FASCINATING DREAM EXPE-
rience although it wasn't the dream itself that impressed
me—it was what happened immediately before I woke
up. I don't remember the content of the dream, but I
heard a voice speaking to me as I was waking. It left me
with the impression that God was talking to me, and
He wanted me to trust him.

I heard a deep and unwavering voice stating, "Trust
in me, and I will take care of all of your problems for you."

Who knows what the voice of God sounds like?
Does He utilize emphatic commands that make us
tremble, or is it that small, quiet voice which the Bible

notes? Can it be either, depending on circumstance? Does He speak to us through the Holy Spirit in a nonverbal way? Does communication need to be with actual words? I believe in nonverbal messages, such as my body tingles and when I feel peace in my heart. I am open to the possibility that his voice presents itself to us in other ways.

My experience with hearing God speaking to me reminded me of one thing: the movie *The Ten Commandments*, starring the actor Charlton Heston. During one scene in the movie, the character Moses is on Mount Sinai, and he approaches the burning bush. The voice that projected from the bush was that of God. Moses was told to remove his sandals because he was standing on holy ground. I heard an identical voice in my dream. I have watched this movie in the past, so it may have influenced how I thought God sounded when He spoke.

I wondered why that message was given to me that morning. Was it because something harmful was going to happen to me and I needed God's help more than ever? I received an answer to that question. Within a few days of hearing the words "trust in me," I had a mammogram appointment. I was deficient in scheduling examinations and had not had one in many years. My healthcare should have been higher on my priority list. I tried to eat well and exercised, but I was overdue when it came to making appointments for tests.

The mammogram I scheduled was a week before I was going away on a trip. I tried taking care of things that needed my attention before I went away on vacation. Completing chores or commitments before I traveled meant I wouldn't have to deal with them after I returned home. Nothing deflated the joy of a vacation faster than being immersed in problems, appointments, housework, or your job after you returned home. How was it possible that a few hours back in the reality of a normal routine could negate a week of pleasure? Sometimes that was what happened. Vacation was more relaxing when I wasn't leaving behind unfinished business that should have received my attention before I departed.

The appointment was not the quick version of show up, test, wait, and leave. It was customary that a woman waited after the exam while a radiologist performed a visual scan of the test images. You could get dressed and leave if nothing obvious was detected. At a later date, the images were reviewed more thoroughly to ensure nothing important was missed, and a report would be sent to you through the mail. On this particular day, the radiology tech told me the test needed to be repeated on one side before I left the building. Something questionable was noted and additional images were requested by the radiologist. I was rescanned and sent back to the waiting area while the new X-rays were reviewed.

The tech returned a second time, and I was told I needed to schedule a follow-up visit; a so-called spot was seen in my left breast. The speck was miniscule, and cancer was not definitely implied, but the radiologist was concerned. He needed to reevaluate me and see if the area in question continued to increase in size. During the next appointment, I would need another scan as well as a breast ultrasound, and a future biopsy might be required. It should not have come as a surprise to me that the test results were abnormal because too much time had elapsed since my last mammogram.

The tech was unable to provide me with further details and didn't offer false reassurances. It took me a moment before I realized that I might have breast cancer. *This could be serious. I feel okay. Why this? Why now?* It was difficult to fathom, but I comprehended one thing: from that point forward, my life could dramatically change. In an instant, life threw me a curveball.

I redressed and walked over to the receptionist to make my next appointment. She offered a couple of available dates as I looked at my calendar. I couldn't believe it—the appointments she suggested were during the middle of my vacation in Yosemite National Park. Perhaps it was ludicrous that I desired to delay the future exam longer than suggested by the radiologist, but I had one thing on my mind: if I was diagnosed with cancer, it would be a long time before I traveled or hiked again in a far-away destination. I wanted one more chance to have an excellent vacation before I received news of a malignancy or endured necessary medical treatments. I scheduled the return appointment for the week after I returned from my trip.

Before I realized it, time progressed forward, and I was in Yosemite. It is a wondrous place, especially in springtime. Wild dogwood trees were blooming, and the waterfalls flowed with massive force. Everywhere I looked were signs of God's tremendous handiwork, and I tried to memorize all of it. I wanted it etched within my mind for eternity. That place was a photographer and nature lover's dream, and I was ecstatic I was there.

Despite all that beauty, there were persistent words that crept into my mind and distracted me: *Repeat test. Biopsy. Breast cancer. Mastectomy. Chemo. Radiation.* I wanted to shake those thoughts from my head. They had no right tagging along with me in that breathtaking national park. When I am on vacation, I don't want to dwell on negative things which may never occur. Why was I allowing my joy to be stolen from me? I was worrying. The awful thing about worrying is that it does not prolong your life by a single day, and it doesn't change the outcome of anything—it only steals precious time from you. I was overthinking a potential cancer diagnosis and became my own worst enemy; I was the culprit who was sabotaging my vacation.

My dream was starting to make sense. I may be faced with a serious health concern, but God wanted me to trust Him and not worry. The voice at the end of the dream also said, "I will take care of all of your problems for you." I could choose to either believe those words or fret about things that I couldn't control. I like to think I have faith in God, but I also have much to learn; exercising faith and trusting God is a perpetual test. Casting our cares to God is a simple concept, but believing in what we profess is difficult when trouble strikes our life. I decided that I was going to place my confidence in God, and I planned on fully enjoying the remainder of my vacation. I wasn't going to torment myself with thoughts about breast cancer any longer.

Each successive day in Yosemite included an incredible hike. On this day, I was going to drive up Glacier Point Road and then hike to an area known as Dewey Point. From that area, I would be able to look down into Yosemite Valley and observe the waterfalls and surrounding peaks from an eagle eye perspective. In order to get to that lookout point, I had to hike through an area known as McGurk Meadows. The open meadows were a direct contrast to the surrounding tall trees and peaks, and a touch of frost coated the native grasses. Birds and animals were often active after sunrise, but I didn't see any of them. I was fond of getting an early start in the morning so I could avoid crowds of tourists, enjoy the serenity of the area, and improve my chances of spotting wildlife. Tranquility ruled the atmosphere, and I should have loved and embraced it. The silence, though, was an invitation to fill my empty mind with thoughts about cancer despite what I had declared about trusting God.

As soon as I realized what I was thinking, I stopped on the trail beside the meadows and looked up toward the crystal-clear blue sky.

I shouted, "No!"

I didn't know why I paused at this precise location, but I needed to break my harmful chain of thoughts. I clung to my dream's powerful and comforting message about trusting God.

I proclaimed, "I will *not* be afraid. I do *not* have cancer. Even if I do, God will take care of me. It will be okay, and I have nothing to worry about!"

God will handle the details and be with me every step of the way. Similar to my hikes, He will provide me with guidance, protection, and strength. I do not have to fear what will happen in the future. God is in control; my only job is to trust Him.

Fortunately, as far as I knew, I was alone on the trail while I spoke those words out loud. Next, I raised my arms straight up in the air and started turning in place in a 360-degree circle while I stared at the sky. It seemed like a natural thing to do at the time. When I was halfway around the circle, I spotted a white feather floating down from the sky. In that windless moment, it gently landed at my feet, and I was astounded. *Where did it come from?* I looked for a bird and neither saw nor heard one as I scanned the treetops. God sent me a clear message that He knew I would understand. A feather affirmed what I spoke while I was in the meadow: everything was going to be okay. I continued my hike with a carefree heart.

I returned home a few days later, and not long after that, the day arrived for my repeat mammogram. As I sat in the waiting room, I looked around, killing time before my test. I noticed a crucifix hanging high on a wall inside the receptionist area. I hoped it provided comfort to whoever noticed it while waiting for testing. The sight of it soothed me, and I prayed until it was my turn for the exam.

The tech asked if there was anyone present who I wanted to join me. It seemed she expected someone to be at my side in case I received bad news and needed emotional support. My husband didn't accompany me to that appointment even though he was aware of the reason for the exam. The hobby shop he owned monopolized his time, and he was the sole employee. Closing the store for half a day wasn't feasible but would have been necessary because it was located forty miles away from the radiology center. I assured him that I didn't require his presence. I was confident I wouldn't receive a cancer diagnosis. I felt armed with all the support I needed, which was from God.

I told the tech, "No."

Once again, a spot was seen on the mammogram;

it hadn't miraculously disappeared. I was led into the next room, and a different tech performed an ultrasound. She verified and then rechecked her paperwork to ensure she was examining the correct side. She scanned both breasts in case the information was wrong. The expression on her face made me curious, so I asked if there was a problem. I was told she couldn't find anything unusual, but she was going to have the doctor on duty take a look. Within minutes, the doctor appeared and performed the ultrasound himself in case the tech's technique was inadequate. He couldn't find the elusive spot either. My questionable cancer speck had mysteriously disappeared; it was undetectable. It was recommended that I continued with six-month mammogram follow-ups until further notice. I needed more frequent monitoring to ensure that nothing returned, grew, or spread.

As I left the medical center, I was elated at the terrific news. To this current date, I haven't had any mammograms which caused concern because they've been normal. I was informed that the spot which was originally noted could have been an inflamed duct or cyst. No one had a concrete explanation for why it was seen on the mammogram but minutes later was unidentifiable by ultrasound. I was satisfied with my own answer: it was God's benevolence and intervention. Trust in God and be grateful for all the miracles He sends your way.

BENEFITS

WHEN WE ASK FOR THINGS OR HELP FROM God, how many of us tell Him how our needs should be met because we have specific ideas in mind? God doesn't operate that way. He has His own plans that are superior to ours. Unfortunately, we are not wise enough to make our requests known and then leave everything else to God. We must resist the urge to dictate to Him how our lives should unfold and how our desires need to be fulfilled.

I periodically go through times when I feel I cannot get organized or accomplish everything I want to complete. I don't know if it's because my to do list is too lengthy or unrealistic. Perhaps I get fatigued due to stress or hypertension and that's why I don't finish tasks. Should I make my needs known and ask others for help? Whatever the case, I thought I was doing the right thing when I asked God for help. While I prayed, I mused about my organizational skills. *Isn't it ironic—it seems I get more done when I have less available free time because I don't dawdle.*

Those words were fresh in my mind when I received a phone call from my manager a couple days later. She notified me that corporate headquarters were changing part-time employee status. That meant that my part-time hours did not meet the newly designated minimums for benefits. I was no longer going to be eligible to receive any health and dental benefits, and I would not accrue any sick or vacation time as of the new year. I was stunned and remained silent. She was sympathetic and explained my options: I could obtain private health insurance, which she already knew was expensive, or I could increase my weekly hours.

In the past, I researched the cost of private health and dental insurance; the premiums and deductibles were astronomical. The plans with the lower premiums had high co-pays and deductibles before the plan contributed toward any care. I tentatively told her I would increase my hours because I didn't see any other feasible option, but I needed to investigate further into insurance plans. I promised to give her a definite answer by the end of the week. It was doubtful I could afford to keep my current work status. One quarter of my biweekly paycheck would have to be allocated toward private healthcare insurance. I needed that money to pay other bills.

When I hung up the phone, my feelings alternated between anger and despair. I burst into tears. *How can they do this to me?* They were doing it to many of us. Regardless of whether an employee had worked for the company for two years or twenty, it didn't matter. We were given a choice that wasn't much of a choice at all. Fortunately, there was a shortage of employees in my department; at least I had the option of increasing my hours to meet the new minimum requirements for benefits. I wondered how many staff members in other areas might be forced to quit because they couldn't afford healthcare costs and weren't allowed to work more hours.

I walked over to my nook table and lit a candle. I prayed to God and said that if this was required to make me more organized, then this was the way it would be. I gave thanks for all the years I worked minimal part-time hours. I asked Him to forgive me if I never said that before or was unappreciative of my former jobs and schedules. I also let God know that if it was His will, I preferred to stay employed with my current schedule. God already knew that, but the Bible told us to pray and make our requests known. I acknowledged that with God all things were possible, and I trusted that He would manage the situation.

At work, I did not like discussing the revamping of part-time status. I was determined to not become upset over the changes that were happening. I'm sure some of my colleagues were secretly pleased that I was going to be forced to work more hours. In the past, I occasionally sensed underlying jealousy because I had a part-time schedule while they worked full time. Now I was going to be one of them. I believed that their voices of concern were ploys to get me to discuss the situation because they knew it distressed me. Some of them may have taken pleasure in my misery. Although I did not say anything because I feared being ridiculed, I believed God was on my side. I was confident He would make the circumstances work out in my favor. Unfortunately, many people don't understand the power of faith.

A fellow part-time employee was trying to convince me to become vocal about the benefit issue. That was not my style, and being loud about it may have caused problems for me in the long run. Fortunately, she sent emails to me that were going to a similar but incorrect email address; I never received any of them. This was confirmed one day at work after she showed me the messages she had sent. I examined the emails and told her she wasn't using my correct address. For an unknown reason, I had been assigned two different email addresses when I began working in the e-ICU. The one I didn't utilize wasn't deleted by the technology department and remained in the healthcare system's email directory.

I had no need to search for my own email address, so I wasn't aware of the error.

I comprehended that God was the only one who could help me. When a corporate entity made an executive decision that affected people, it was not created without considerable thought. Financial ramifications were a priority and were always in their own favor. A company didn't back down and reverse a decision because of a few outspoken employees. Take it or leave it was the mentality. We would be replaced if we quit. The corporate hierarchy didn't care if the people who were affected by the benefit changes were dissatisfied.

I prayed on a daily basis—or whenever I needed additional inner strength, which was often. The Thanksgiving and Christmas season was approaching. I worked on becoming more organized in anticipation of having fewer free non-working hours after the new year. Another one of my goals was to maintain the best possible attitude toward my employment situation. I refrained from feeling sorry for myself and my circumstance. There are countless numbers of people in this world who work longer hours for less pay or who work multiple jobs out of necessity.

An explanation wasn't given when, days later, the new rules regarding part-time employees were abolished and I was returned to the category of status quo. Upon hearing the message from my manager, I was in disbelief. After my phone conversation with her ended,

I wept as hard as when I received the negative news. I shed tears of joy, relief, and thankfulness.

I dropped to my knees and shouted, "With God, *all* things are possible!"

Who else but God changed the minds of professional management? God was merciful to me and the non-union, part-time employees of that company. *Hallelujah!*

If there was ever a day to be grateful for God's intervention in my life, that was it. Were those few weeks a test of my reliance on Him to fix what was broken in my life? Perhaps. Regardless, those weeks of faith led to increased faith. He remedied an obvious cause of anxiety in my life without any interference on my part. Thank you, God; that was awesome.

GREENFIELD

WHENEVER I HAVE AN INTENSE DREAM THAT inspires me or gives me direction, I wake up feeling that something special has touched my life. I love dreams that seem to indicate I'm on the correct path toward a beneficial outcome. Who doesn't enjoy receiving encouragement or perceiving that they are doing the right thing? Occasionally, I experience dreams that are cautionary messages. They emphasize a behavior I need to change, or they teach me some other lesson.

I question why these messages often utilize serpents. I have had many dreams which *don't* involve snakes, but the majority of noteworthy ones I've had do include them. I am certain that a psychologist may have a symbolic or rational explanation. God communicates with me in any manner He chooses. Snakes emphasize the point He wants to make, and the message is explicit.

In this particular dream, I was walking along a downtown street of a small community that I was familiar with as a child. I strolled with someone who I presumed was a friend or acquaintance; I never saw their face in the dream. We were window shopping and enjoying the day when we noticed storm clouds that were building from the west. Other people observed them too. The atmosphere of the entire street was transformed in an instant as fear and tension filled the air. We looked around and realized everyone had departed. They disappeared into various shops, and we were the only ones left on the sidewalk. Pouring rain and intense lightning were headed our way. The foul weather was going to envelop us. We made a split-second decision and darted into a nearby store where we would wait until the storm passed.

Within moments, I knew we made a wrong and frightening decision. The shop where we sought shelter was one that I don't believe I ever would have stepped into except by sheer accident. The store sold paraphernalia that related to witchcraft and voodoo. A palpable feeling of evil existed in the gloomy interior. I wanted to flee from that place. It would be safer riding out the storm on the street than to remain surrounded by the demonic presence that I felt inside that building. I couldn't escape it fast enough.

Before I could locate a door and reach the exit, a figure in dark clothing came at me and brandished a snake in a threatening manner. I guessed the serpent was poisonous or lethal, and the person took pleasure in taunting me with it. He laughed at my level of discomfort with his and the snake's proximity to me. I was cornered. *What can I do? How do I get out of this situation?* I did the only thing which I knew could help: I called out to Jesus.

"Jesus, I know you will help me, and no harm will come to me because of you. I know you will protect me and keep me safe!"

My voice could be heard throughout the store, and others took notice of what I was yelling. Despite the fact that the man was waving the snake inches from my face, I was not hurt. The sinister being departed and sought others he could frighten.

Although I was relieved that the immediate threat was removed from my presence, I was disheartened by the reaction of the crowd of people who were in the store. They were unbelievers and ridiculed me. They also started blaspheming God and the name of Jesus. I urgently wanted to leave the area because I was outnumbered and they started circling around me. I was terrified of the menacing mob and wondered how I was going to escape from my predicament. I prayed again for assistance from Jesus, and within moments, my fear was transformed into strength.

Without realizing what I was doing, I stretched my arm out toward an obnoxious individual who was standing across from me. His obscenities and ruthless jeering were more than I could bear. He mocked me repeatedly for invoking the name of Jesus and crying to Him for help. In a microsecond of rage, I flicked my wrist and pointed at him. Volts of energy flew from my fingertip, which struck the man and sent him flying to the ground. I don't know whether the lightning bolts that originated from my hand were visible to anyone except me, but the effect was undeniable.

I shouted, "How *dare* you doubt the name and power of Jesus!"

The man I targeted was knocked unconscious and remained motionless on the floor.

I heard a collective gasp, and then everyone who surrounded me dropped to their knees and bowed their heads. Miraculously, the angry mob was converted to Christianity. They abandoned their witchcraft and occult beliefs and became believers in the one true God.

The dream was fascinating up until this point, but it was not over. As the dream continued, I stood and observed the crowd as they kneeled on the floor. A solitary figure approached me. She had been lurking a short distance away in a dim corner of the store. I started to fear her as much as the man with the snake. She was dressed in long layers of ebony clothing, and much of the fabric trailed behind her as she walked. I knew without asking that she was the owner of the shop and was probably irate over what had just occurred. At the very least, she was going to tell me to leave, but I expected that she wanted to physically harm me.

Her actions surprised me more than the lightning bolts that emanated from my fingertip. She leaned toward me and whispered into my ear, "You discovered and used something they never knew about until now. There is power when you invoke the name of Jesus. Nothing can prevail against him. You were very fortunate, indeed, because you already learned and heeded that message." She silently withdrew from me and allowed me to leave.

The unshakeable images of the snake, the shop owner, and the intimidating crowd have remained with me for years. The dream is confirmation of everything I believe—there *is* power in Jesus's name, and He is available to intercede on our behalf when we pray and ask for help. No situation is too difficult that God or Jesus cannot help us. Trusting Him and accepting His son is the only way we need to live. Even though I dislike snakes, I'd rather experience one of those dreams over a thousand waking hours spent in darkness and confusion without God.

I hope that each of you someday receives a miraculous affirmation dream from God, because when you have one, you feel truly blessed.

SEPTEMBER THIRD

WHEN I WOKE UP ON THE FINAL DAY OF MY dog's life, I didn't know it was going to be her last. Daisy seemed ill, so I made a vet appointment. She appeared to have been deteriorating over the past couple of days for some unknown reason, which was why I sought care for her. I didn't want to wait until her sickness became an emergency, which most likely would have occurred at an inconvenient time. I suppose it is never convenient being ill, but we can take action sooner rather than later.

Daisy's appointment was not until late in the day, which was not unexpected. I preferred Dr. Laura, and she usually worked afternoons until closing hour. This gave me all day to spend with the doggie before I learned that she had developed some problem that was critical, chronic, or easily cured. I decided to spend the day wisely. There was a real possibility that she was going to die that day, but I did not want to waste it by crying and remaining in a depressed state inside my home. The dog was not going to understand my sorrow. I needed to comfort her since she was not feeling well instead of the other way around. Animals can be stoics and will put aside their own pain to please their masters. How fortunate we are to have such creatures in our lives. They deserve to be loved and treated well.

I was determined to spend a day of normalcy with Daisy, which included an abundant amount of love. I didn't know with certainty that she was going to die, and part of my routine was to go out and exercise for a short while by myself. I usually rode my bicycle or went for a walk. I knew that walking and talking to God would fortify and prepare me for what I may face later that day.

My prayer to God was simple: His will be done, regardless of what that included. I offered my dog to Him, similar to what I said when my previous dog was sick. I don't own my dog; I'm simply a custodian until God decides He wants her back. That is true with people too. We never know when God will call us back to Him, which is why every day we live should be appreciated and considered precious.

The small miracle that I experienced that day

occurred after the completion of my walk. Regardless of how I exercised, after I returned home, I took Daisy outside with me so she could also enjoy fresh air. It was often midday by the time I got back to the house, so I had to spend time with Daisy under the shade of a tree. She wasn't especially tolerant of heat, which was true of most bulldogs. The shade made being outside comfortable for her, as long as she wasn't exerting herself. She was becoming prone to panting from sunrise to sunset; she only stopped from sheer exhaustion. I brought her outside with me as usual because she was going to breathe rapidly whether she was inside the house or in the yard. I laid a beach towel on the ground for her next to my chair, which was underneath a young oak tree. We were close to a small landscaped area with a perennial flower garden and a birdfeeder hung from a pole attached to a nearby tree. This was one of my favorite spots in the yard because it was next to a magnolia tree that I had planted in memory of my beloved white bulldog.

Unfortunately, Daisy was unable to relax during that sun-filled afternoon. She continually panted, and my heart was breaking for the sweet dog who was always excited to be outside with me in the past. Daisy was unable to lie down on the towel and have a nap due to her discomfort. She was uninterested in the birds, chipmunks, and squirrels; she used to watch their antics. I attempted reading a book, but my mind was focused on her. I tried not to be pessimistic about her prognosis.

As my mind wandered, I noticed the birds who came to the tree branches above our heads. The birds never seemed too disturbed by our presence a few feet away from the feeder, but they mainly stayed in the woods until it was time to get a quick snack. After they grabbed a seed, they retreated back to the larger trees until it was time to repeat their pattern of feeding and flying away. This day, their behavior seemed strange to me. They were closer to us than usual, and when I looked up into the overhead branches, I saw feathered heads with tiny eyes that peered down at me and Daisy. It was a common theme for the afternoon—different varieties of birds flew into this one particular tree, waited for a short while, and then continued to the feeder. Chickadees, nuthatches, tufted titmice, and cardinals all participated in this procession. They should have been frightened by the loudly panting dog, but they seemed to exude love, not fear. It was as if one by one they came to say goodbye to Daisy and bid her farewell. She never harassed the birds; instead, she did them a favor when she chased away ravenous squirrels who aggressively hogged the bird food for themselves. The simple but unusual act of the birds visiting low branches and seemingly bidding adieu to my lovable bulldog confirmed one thing to me: my dog was going to die that day. God sent me a miraculous sign that gently informed me about what was going to happen.

We went back inside the house after a couple of

hours. Perhaps she might have wanted some food or fresh cold water, but she could not eat or drink. While we tried relaxing on the soft sofa, I picked up a book that I purchased regarding the promises of God. I resumed reading from my last bookmarked page and was astounded by the verse which was in front of me: "Yea, though I walk through the valley of the shadow of death, I will fear no evil, for thou art with me." That verse reminded me of funerals, and it was supposed to be reassuring. I repeated that scripture to Daisy, although I knew she didn't understand what it meant. The words spoke clearly to me and reiterated the sentiment from the fearless birds who visited us. God knows how to individually communicate with each of us in a way we understand. It is up to us to open our hearts and minds and take note of what He has to say.

Yes, Daisy died that day, on September third. She had a large abdominal tumor as well as neurologic symptoms, which suggested she might have also had brain cancer. Her prognosis was poor and additional testing and treatment would not have changed the eventual outcome. I didn't want her to endure further suffering; she was euthanized and died peacefully.

My belief in God did not spare me from crying and feeling anguish over her death, but it helped me remember she was a temporary gift. I was blessed by having known her, even if it was for little over a year. God sent her to me so both of us could experience love and she would be tenderly cared for during her last year of life. Everything happens for a reason. She arrived in and departed from my life according to God's plans for me. I was grateful for the serene final afternoon I spent with Daisy, which included God's precious birds and words as sources of love and comfort.

FLUTE

I OFTEN THOUGHT ABOUT MY FIRST VACA-
tion to Sedona, and I hoped my upcoming trip to that
region would be as spiritual and exciting. Undoubtedly,
it would be picturesque and fascinating in Sedona's
own unparalleled way. I wondered, though, if I would
once again feel a special bond with God while I was
there; a slower pace may help with that. Vacations are
packed with so much to see and do because we don't
want to omit anything, but we sometimes pay a price:
we are more exhausted after vacation than before it
begins. We end up missing something on our trips—the
peacefulness which comes from connecting with God
when we quiet our minds and absorb the beauty that
surrounds us.

I was not disappointed with my first day of hiking. Although I started later than usual, I guessed that it must have been for a reason. I wanted to see a vortex site and splendid canyon that I missed on my first trip, so I headed toward Boynton Canyon. The side spur off the main trail to the concentrated vortex location was short and scenic. I felt relaxed as I headed toward a rock bench near the vortex pinnacle. I thanked God for the magnificence that surrounded me and for getting me to Sedona safely. The ledge where I sat down was in a serene area, and I attempted to absorb the atmosphere of the entire place.

A couple of tourists arrived at the site and saw me gulping a large quantity of water that I retrieved from my backpack. We began a conversation, and I learned they were from Massachusetts. We discussed noteworthy features in Sedona as well as the coincidence of meeting someone else on vacation who lived close to their home state. Before they departed, they asked me about the man who played the wind flute at the vortex site. They wondered if I knew when he appeared and played his solo concert and if he actually climbed to the apex of the rock formation. I said I never heard about him but that it must be entertaining when you saw or heard his impromptu recitals.

I began heading back to the main trail junction after I was done resting. I passed by several friendly people. There were groups of men and women as well as singles and couples. A solitary gentleman and I exchanged greetings with each other. He extended his arm toward me and opened his hand.

"I'd like to give you a healing heart from Mother Earth."

He presented me with a unique heart-shaped rock. I accepted it and traced the shape of the rock with a finger as it rested in my palm.

I couldn't resist smiling and inquired, "Did you find this, or do you carve rocks?"

He grinned as he replied, "I like to think that they find me."

I kept the rock and placed it in the pocket of my shorts. "Thank you so much. I hope you have a lovely day."

Not long after we each proceeded on our individual hikes in opposite directions, I pondered the unusual encounter with the stranger. He gave me a one of a kind present and asked for nothing in return. I considered if he was a New Age believer or possibly a Native American. Did it matter? He didn't try to convert me to whatever beliefs he holds dear. Sometimes a gift is just a gift. Why do we gravitate toward believing someone else has ulterior motives? I decided to believe the best of him, not the worst. He shared peace and joy with me. God works through people to do those types of things for us. Perhaps this was God's way of providing me with a healed heart after the loss of my dog Daisy.

God created everything in the universe, including that rock; I felt it was a gift from the Creator himself.

I clung to and meditated on God's peace, love, and unimaginable treasures until the haunting sounds of a wind flute interrupted my thoughts. I stopped abruptly in my tracks when I heard the musical instrument's tune as it drifted toward me along the canyon trail. I turned back to the vortex site and saw the silhouetted figure of a man playing a flute. The vision of him backlit by the morning sun combined with the melody he played was mesmerizing. The mystery man who gave me the heart rock was the infamous flute player. His timing was incredible, and it felt like he was serenading me. I wondered if he saw me standing on the trail, listening to his music. I hoped that it brought him joy knowing someone wasn't in a hurry and appreciated the gifts he shared with others. Several minutes later, I resumed hiking. Additional grandeur on the trail waited to be discovered and explored. As I proceeded, I was in awe over the length of time I heard the flute and how its sweet tune was carried throughout the canyon.

Did I end up seeing all the other sites I planned on visiting that day? Of course not. I found what I was looking for first thing that morning: the serenity that came when you slowed down and appreciated life as well as what God created. The hike was delightful, and it was a glorious day.

I desired tranquility and found it. At the very least, I resurrected peace that I knew already dwelled inside of me. I asked God for a fantastic vacation and safe hiking. He provided both of these things and much more. Seek God first and then all good and necessary things will be provided to those who ask.

CATHEDRAL ROCK

AN ACTIVITY THAT WAS ON MY AGENDA THE second time I visited Sedona was a hike up Cathedral Rock. It was another concentrated vortex area. The sight of this rock formation from its base was gorgeous, but I longed to see the views from among its upper spires.

What motivated me to ascend that rock the most was the fact that I didn't successfully climb it during my first trip. I tried scrambling up it once, but my doubts and fears got the best of me. Until you attempted that trail yourself, no book or person could prepare you for what you encountered. The statistics say that the trail is three-quarters of a mile in length with an elevation gain of 750 feet. Those are not staggering figures for anyone who exercises regularly or even someone like me who hikes infrequently.

Included in the description of the trail found in a guidebook were words of caution: "Beware if you fear tenuous footing or are afraid of heights." *Hmmm...that part leaves a lot to the imagination.*

I understood within minutes what that meant after I attempted hiking that trail during my last vacation to Sedona. I didn't hike far up Cathedral Rock before I stopped and retreated to the safety of its base. Two things dominated my mind that prompted me to abandon that hike. I believed the notion that I might slip, fall, and die. If I made it to my destination, I had to complete a fearful and treacherous descent before the day was over.

Prior to my second vacation to Sedona, I contemplated my inability to hike to the end of the Cathedral Rock Trail. I considered what I did wrong, what went through my mind at the time, and what I could have done differently. Older and younger people who appeared less physically fit than me were hiking that trail. Children of various ages climbed past me with ease. I was embarrassed that I gave up so easily. I was determined to hike this trail because I wanted to erase my previous failure.

What I felt I had on my side this time was God. Two years had transpired since I was in Sedona, and I felt I had grown in faith as a Christian. I knew God protected me on the trails, and I embraced a couple of mottos, which I recited. My first mantra was, "I will do my best, and God will do the rest." As long as I tried with earnest effort, I knew God would help me succeed. Additionally, I considered scripture and repeated to myself, "I can do all things through Christ, who strengthens me." With an attitude like that, how could I possibly fail?

Early on a Sunday morning, I drove to the Cathedral Rock trailhead. The angle of the rising sun illuminated the rocks in a stunning manner. I took a few photographs as well as several deep breaths as I approached the bottom of the rock structure. *This is it. Here we go.* Besides reiterating the two phrases I adopted, I threw in a couple "Our Father" prayers for good measure.

The beginning of the trail was exactly as I remembered: it began with a moderate incline then steadily gained altitude. There were vague nooks in the rocks that were supposed to be hand or footholds. I was able to overcome the tricky area that caused me to abandon my initial attempt up Cathedral Rock. The difficult footing was ceaseless, and I was faced with a steep crevice that baffled me. I could not figure out how you climbed up through that area. I stood and stared at it and demanded that an answer of how to scale it needed to come screaming at me from the rocks—all I heard was silence. My mind began filling with my own voice and nagging doubts.

A decision needed to be made at that point. I needed

to either withdraw from the trail once again or miraculously find the strength to continue. I was dejected because I felt like an overwhelming failure. Although I proceeded further than the first time I tried that hike, it was little consolation. Worse yet, from my vantage point, I saw other people who started ascending the trail. Upon arriving at my location, they would either have to wait for me to proceed or attempt to squeeze past me on a dangerous ledge. I would be the cause of a congested bottle neck on a narrow part of the trail. Without delay, I needed to choose whether to go up or down the rock.

Help me, God. Help me. You know what I want, but I don't know what I should do. Please tell me what to do.

Meanwhile, as I waited for an answer from God because the rocks were not willing to provide one, the first person below me reached my location. It was a young lady in neon pink athletic shorts who was running up the trail. As she approached, I tried creating space that allowed her to squeeze by me.

"I'll let you go past me while I decide whether I want to continue up the trail or not. If I'm ahead of you, I'll slow you down."

She lessened her speed and asked if I had ever hiked this trail. I admitted that I tried once before and made more progress than the first time but that my fears were going to prevent me from going any further. After I said that to her, I turned around and was about to proceed back down the rocks. She understood my trepidation and, without hesitating, offered to take me to the highest point of the trail. I couldn't believe my ears. *Did she actually offer to help me get to the top?* I thanked her for her offer but acknowledged that I was a slow hiker; I didn't want to waste her time. She was persistent and told me she didn't feel like running up the trail that day; she could use me as her excuse for a more leisurely pace. She had stopped running and urged me to join her.

"Come on, you can do it. We'll get to the top. I'll show you the way."

She introduced herself as Natalie and was full of positive energy and optimism. Before I had a chance and made more excuses or thought about what I was doing, I started following the path she took. I hiked about six feet behind her most of the way and remained focused on the back of her heels. She kept me engaged in conversation, which was laden with words of encouragement. I appreciated her enthusiasm, genuine kindness, and selflessness for what she was doing for me. Natalie's pace was reasonable, and she stepped confidently along the route. Her devotion to ensuring I made it to the summit was remarkable.

Within a brief span of time, we were at the end of the trail. We hadn't stopped for any breaks or photo opportunities, which was fine with me. We were on a mission and made it to our destination in what seemed like mere minutes. *How did we get to the top?* One moment, I was paralyzed by fear as I stood and looked up at the spires; in the next instant, I was on a small mesa high up among them. It was a successful journey due to the presence of a young woman who wanted to give a solo hiker an incredible experience.

I thanked her profusely and admitted with the utmost sincerity, "Natalie, I couldn't have done it without you."

As she turned to depart, I remembered that I had a twenty-dollar bill in a side pocket inside my camera case. I asked her to wait for a minute as I retrieved the bill and tried handing it to her. She was surprised but refused to take it. I hoped I wasn't insulting Natalie by offering her money. I told her I wanted to give her something in return because she facilitated an adventure that was priceless. It was a small token of my appreciation for her assistance. Perhaps she could buy herself a refreshing sports drink and snack or put it toward future athletic gear. Without taking the cash, she smiled, waved goodbye, and began running down the trail.

Shortly after she departed, a gentleman who had been climbing behind us greeted me on the mesa.

"You did good keeping up with her. She usually runs up this trail."

He insinuated that I was in fairly good shape because maintaining her pace fatigued most people. He was a local resident who walked this trail on a daily basis and was familiar with Natalie. I valued his comments because I felt unfit and was seconds away from another failed attempt of this hike before I met the young runner.

Despite being a weekend morning, there were few people on the summit. The couples and lone gentleman who were there soon descended, and I was left by myself. I sat down on a rock next to a gnarled juniper tree and admired the views. The place was astounding, and I listened to two canyon wrens who sang to each other. One was perched in the tree next to me, and the other was hidden among the rock spires. It was difficult imagining that I was blessed with solitude at that popular site. I was alone for an hour and spent that time absorbing the experience. I wanted it imprinted in my mind for eternity.

What impressed me the most about this trail was Natalie's arrival at my side. God sent me a real-life angel when I needed one. Her appearance at the right moment and assistance was a miracle. I guessed she was twenty-five years younger than me. Why on earth would a physically fit woman want to assist a shabbily dressed hiker to whom she owed nothing? I purposely wore my worst shorts in anticipation of slipping or sliding on my butt down the rocks. Both the heat of the day and my nerves made me perspire profusely. I thought my stench alone would have made her want to run away from me at breakneck speed. Instead, she generously offered her knowledge, enthusiasm, and climbing skills. She assisted a stranger and gave someone a unique and valuable experience. It was God's fantastic timing that allowed me to proceed up the trail. He worked through a thoughtful person and answered my prayers. It was affirmation that our prayers were heard, and God blessed those who believed in him.

Weeks later, I continued thinking about that outstanding hike and Natalie's assistance. When I closed my eyes, I pictured an imaginary piece of rope. One end was tied around her waist, and the other was secured around mine. It was as if there truly was an invisible rope that God provided, and she used to supernaturally drag me up the trail. Although the hike was not effortless, I was given the gift of sure-footed steps and stamina. I heaved my own weight and backpack up steep rocks. I was in awe of that exceptional day and God's powerful hand, which led me to my desired destination. Thank you, God. I tried my best, and when I hesitated, you provided a guide and did the rest. Your miracles never cease to amaze me.

NAVARRO

I LOVED IT WHEN GOD SENT ME DELICATE feathers, and He knew they brought me joy. I found feathers at my feet while hiking. At home, they were in my hair when I woke up in the morning, or they floated down from the sky. They mysteriously appeared when I was deep in thought or tried making difficult decisions. I wanted to think I discovered them, but they seemed to locate me. It reminded me of how the Sedona flute player told me those heart-shaped rocks found him. The feathers pulled me closer to God because I believed it was His way of acknowledging my thoughts and prayers—but God was weaning me from them. Discovering a feather became a rare event. I had to rely strictly on the intangible means when I had questions and needed answers. The Bible stated there was a time and purpose for everything under the sun. I was certain that my days of receiving feathers were over.

I learned to be satisfied with merely seeing or hearing the birds themselves. I appreciated them whether they were on the ground or in the air and graced me with their presence. I enjoyed the times when I was in close proximity with birds even though I wasn't finding individual feathers anymore. I chuckled to myself. *The birds need their feathers more than I do—they belong to and should remain on the birds.*

Those thoughts permeated my mind as I spent an afternoon shopping in Sedona. Not far from the center of town, there was an outdoor mall full of upscale shops. Interesting and beautiful items were sold there; the choices were overwhelming. There were copious amounts of jewelry and almost anything else with a southwestern theme. I loved the art, trinkets, and home goods I saw. The aromas that came from the nearby restaurants added to the atmosphere as I strolled among the shops. I cautiously determined what I wanted to buy because it would be easy to spend more than my budget allowed. I preferred to buy a few high-quality items rather than a multitude of cheaper things. In order to minimize impulse purchases, I looked at a piece I fancied then walked away to another store. The delay caused me to seriously consider if it was something I truly wanted.

A pricey item which I spotted and immediately desired was a piece of art by Chris Navarro. He is an award-winning artist from Wyoming. Chris Navarro specializes in bronze sculptures with western, wildlife, or inspirational themes. He produced commissioned sculptures that were both life size and monumental size. Within his galleries, customers can find sculptures that are more suitable for the interior of a person's home. I was fond of his artwork called "Mother's Pride." It was a charming sculpture that consisted of a mountain lion and her two kittens. I never previously saw anything that captured the tough but tender essence of a mother mountain lion. The sculpture was a quality piece that I wanted displayed in my home. I planned on placing it underneath an attractive painting that I commissioned from a southwestern artist years ago. I knew I would treasure that sculpture from the Navarro gallery. Even though I was excited about the potential purchase, I walked away for about an hour, but I returned to the gallery before it closed for the evening. I was relieved that the weighty sculpture I bought was going to be shipped to my home. It would be insured, carefully packed, and more likely to make it to the East Coast unmarred than if I toted it myself. As I was giving the employee my shipping address, I noted an object on the checkout counter. I was astonished and stopped speaking in mid-sentence.

I picked up the piece of art and uttered, "Uh, I'll take this too."

It was a replica of an eagle feather that was cast in bronze. The solitary feather was carved with great detail. The bronze gave it weight, but it looked as though it gracefully floated down from the sky and landed in the store. Now it was mine.

I wasn't looking for ornamental feather objects or jewelry, although they were plentiful in southwestern shops. I leisurely shopped and wasn't searching for anything in particular. I surprised myself when I bought the lion sculpture because I didn't collect major pieces of art. The oil painting from California was an exception.

Finding the bronze eagle feather was not a coincidence. I believed that God directed me into that art gallery because He knew I would behold something that brought me immense joy. God provided me with a permanent substitute for the feathers I encountered over the years. It is a lasting reminder of His love for me and a nearly indestructible piece of work that rests in my home. It was incredible how God led me to that special token.

When we show our dedication and love to God instead of embracing material things, He often blesses us with something better than what we imagine for ourself. I thanked God for the splendid feathers He sent my way in the past. The hardy bronze one, though, surpassed them all.

HOLY CROSS

MY LAST DAY OF HIKING IN SEDONA PROVED to be as fascinating as the first. Unlike my hikes earlier that week, I was determined to visit several easy trails versus a fairly long or more strenuous one. Each morning, I had hoped to hike more than one trail, but those plans were too ambitious. Instead, I hiked at a slower pace and became engrossed in what each trail had to offer. I scanned scenic red rock formations while I enjoyed the warmth of the sun on my face. I valued the silence, which was interspersed with the sounds of melodic or chattering birds. There was no need to rush, and I was content although I did not get to visit everything I wanted to see. Often, I succumbed to the heat of the day, the elevation of the area, or the weight of my backpack. Since I had reached my last day of vacation, I was motivated to explore the remaining trails on my agenda.

My usual routine was to start hiking early in the day before the weather became hot. I hiked my first trail without difficulty, but I almost stepped on a snake while admiring the views. Fortunately, it wasn't a rattlesnake but a docile and nonvenomous creature. I should have been paying attention to my footing. Usually, I was more cautious. The majority of my hiking experience was in New England, and I was aware that loose rocks or roots that protruded from the ground could make you trip and fall. There weren't as many hazards on the trails in Sedona, so I had become lax. The best views weren't underneath your feet; they were ahead of or behind you. I looked around and noted how scenes could rapidly change and were affected by the angles of the sun.

Little Horse was the next trail I wanted to hike. The parking lot for that trail was the one I used when I accessed the Courthouse Loop via the Bell Rock pathway. I passed the Little Horse Spur Trail earlier that week and considered I may make it back to that location. One thing that caused me to avoid that section in the past, even though I was told it was beautiful, was the notion of the jeep tours I might encounter. I didn't ask enough questions regarding the jeep adventures. I pictured how I would be hiking and encounter a vehicle loaded with tourists. I imagined loud microphones, smelly exhaust fumes, and people who wanted a snapshot and got in the way of my peaceful enjoyment of the area. I considered myself blessed that I had two legs on which I walked and examined trails at any speed I desired. There was a need for jeep tours for people who otherwise wouldn't see what I saw. I felt that many individuals didn't make the effort to walk; they wanted to take the effortless way over a trail. It's unfortunate that they don't realize what they are missing. Earlier in the week, I saw a couple pedestrians who looked up at the sky as a noisy helicopter tour passed overhead. The gentleman pointed to the ground and told me in his German accent that he liked to see things the old-fashioned way. I wholeheartedly agreed with him.

My fears about the trail being overcrowded were squelched. I only encountered a few mountain bikers and people on foot, but the majority of the time I was by myself. I appreciated the solitude because it gave me plenty of time to think. My mind wandered as I reviewed the events of the week: individual trails I had visited, the unique experiences of the days, and the quiet nights at the cabin. Overall, it was a fantastic vacation, and I couldn't envision it being any better than it was.

Considering my recent snake encounter, I was more careful about watching my steps. I mused about the innumerable rocks along the trail including those which passed under my feet. I pondered this trail as well as others I had hiked. Rocks provided information about the terrain on which I traveled. Though the years, I have seen rocks in a myriad of shapes, textures, and colors, but I never spotted a rock which resembled the shape of a heart. My thoughts drifted back to my first hike that week and the mysterious flute player's gift of the healing heart rock. Subconsciously, from that day forward, I found myself obsessed with rocks. I hoped I would find a heart-shaped stone myself. Many different figures were noted, but none of them resembled a heart.

Oh well. I suppose I needed to remain contented with the prized rock I received as a gift.

As I continued along the trail and marveled at the scenery, I spotted the Chapel of the Holy Cross in the distance. The chapel is a Catholic church that contrasts the metaphysical spiritual beliefs of the area. It sits among the red rocks at the base of a 1500-feet high cliff and was built on Coconino National Forest land. A ninety-foot-tall iron cross is located on the southwestern wall of the church, and it contributes to its aesthetic value. The church was completed in 1956 and is on the National Register of Historic Places.

I knew the path I was on was supposed to intersect with the Chapel Trail and a few others. I stopped and looked in awe at the chapel. It was strategically situated among the massive rocks, and the simple design was attractive. Unlike the view of the chapel from its access road where I took photos earlier that week, the vantage point from the trail put its size into perspective. I wanted to take photos of it from that location to show friends the chapel and its scale compared to the surrounding cliffs.

Before I retrieved my camera out of its protective bag, I meditated in the spot where I stood. At that time, one phrase started repeating in my mind: *At the name of Jesus, every knee should bend, and every head should bow.* How could one not show respect and appreciation for the huge holy cross that loomed in the distance? I thanked God for keeping me safe during my journey. I expressed my gratitude to Jesus for interceding on my behalf when I prayed and for being my savior. Despite the fact that it was a splendid day, I was on the verge of tears.

I took photos from various angles then decided it was time to continue up the trail. Before I proceeded, I wanted to place my camera back in its case, which was strapped around my waist. I preferred carrying the camera in this fashion; the weight of it hanging from around my neck sometimes gave me neck pain after a brief period of time. My favorite camera, which I brought with me on vacation, was a hefty professional Nikon, and the wide angle zoom lens added weight to it. As I looked down and nestled the camera in its bag, I noticed an odd rock at my feet—it appeared to be a heart-shaped rock. When I picked it up and held it, I wept. Indeed, it *was* a heart-shaped rock!

I examined the front and back of the rock. On one side of it was a hairline crack at the top. When I flipped it to the opposite side, the rock was whole and without blemish, as if it was healed. I favored the unmarred side, and it rested on my palm the way I originally held the rock from the flute player.

I had hiked many miles of trails over the years and spent countless hours in the mountains, deserts, and wilderness. Moments after I meditated upon the holy cross of Jesus, I spotted a heart-shaped rock—it was a deliberate and loving gift from God.

FIONA

HOW MANY PEOPLE IN THIS WORLD QUES-
tion or are angry with God? When things don't go our
way or live up to our expectations, it's easy to blame
God. The worst offenders who question God are possibly, but not limited to, Christians. We feel that, as
believers, God should protect us from the evil incidents
and accidents of this world. Why are we betrayed with
tragedy, illness, or loss if we are faithful, church-going
people? Why, God, why? How can this happen? When
are you going to help me? I thought you loved me!
Those were a few of the phrases most people have
probably said at one point or another in their life.
When we ask those questions, it's likely in an angry
and accusatory tone, without regard for God's master

plan for our life. We were never promised a carefree life, but after we placed our trust in God, we felt He owed that to us in return.

There haven't been many times I've questioned God's authority over matters in my life. I've lived by believing that everything happens for a reason. Yes, sometimes I'd like answers to my questions of why things have happened to me, but I tried not to ask in a rebellious or sarcastic tone. I thought I might find peace in the answers and felt I could accept whatever rationale I received. It is important to understand, though, that God isn't obliged to give us answers—He doesn't need to explain anything to us. God reveals whatever He wants us to know according to His own desires and timing.

After my bulldog Daisy died, my heart ached for multiple reasons over that loss. My husband and I had her as a pet for barely over a year. In that brief amount of time, I fell in love with Daisy and her quirky and fun-loving nature. She was a good girl who brought humor to our lives, and that hefty dog's easygoing personality would be missed.

What hurt me the most was the fact that I had agreed with my husband that after Daisy died, we would not obtain any future pets. There would be no more dogs, regardless of whether they were puppies or adults. When I agreed to his request at the beginning of Daisy's life with us, I had no way of knowing she was going to be ours for barely fifteen months. I didn't expect her to die so soon. Even if the shelter personnel underestimated her age by a few months or a couple of years, I expected she would live for at least three more years. I'm guessing that owning her for three years would have satisfied me, but learning to love an animal and then to lose them so soon was brutal. I couldn't believe I was once again facing loneliness after the loss of a beloved pet.

Wayne's reasons for not wanting another dog made sense. Caring for a pet required sacrifices in both time and money. A pet was dependent on their owner for their lifetime. They needed someone reliable who provided them with food, shelter, healthcare, and companionship. I didn't complain, but I cringed whenever I handed over my credit card and paid an annual veterinary bill. The charges included the office visit fee, vaccinations, tests, and monthly preventative medication. Pet food prices were steadily increasing, but proper nutrition was essential in order to keep a dog healthy. Dogs shouldn't be left alone for endless hours either. They needed outdoor bathroom breaks to relieve their bladder or bowels. Animals get lonely too and can develop destructive behaviors or anxiety issues without companionship. We didn't want to pay for doggie daycare. Neither did we desire having a pet sitter in our home. His arguments were all valid, but I believed the obligations and expenses were offset by the love you received from a pet.

Fortunately, I had already planned my second trip to Sedona that fall; it was a tremendous vacation and a welcomed distraction—except when I saw other people hiking with their dogs in the cool morning air. It made me downcast at times, but it was also heartwarming when I witnessed a carefree dog enjoying the outdoors with their master. The healing heart rock that I was given reminded me of Daisy. It felt like a gift sent from her in heaven. It let me know she was okay and that euthanizing her distressed me a lot more than it hurt her.

When I returned home from Sedona, it didn't take long for those feelings of loneliness to return. The emptiness of the house engulfed me while Wayne was at work. I tried enjoying my new-found freedom, but I couldn't. I had owned dogs for a total of nineteen years, and I imagined I experienced what parents whose children went away to college initially underwent—empty nest syndrome. My dogs were as real to me as any two-legged child was to a parent. All of my fur-babies were now gone, and I was no longer a pet's mama. I wanted to rescue another dog.

During my breaks at work, I couldn't resist looking at rescue or shelter websites. I searched for a young adult English bulldog. Most of the local dogs I viewed were mixed breeds and didn't fit my criteria. Perhaps that was a good thing. I didn't want to rescue anything other than a purebred bulldog; I was familiar with that breed and preferred that type of dog. I had mixed emotions while viewing those websites. I wanted to obey my husband's wishes, but at the same time, I felt cheated out of a pet's companionship. It wasn't fair. I wasn't ready to spend my days alone and missed talking to a dog or having one ecstatically greet me when I arrived home. I wanted a faithful furry pal who would learn to adore me.

Shortly before Halloween, I located a female rescue dog named Fiona who needed a permanent home. I filled out the adoption paperwork online. If I received a response regarding the application, I would speak to Wayne about it. I felt uneasy with the way I was going about the situation because I was sneaking around behind his back. Regardless, I convinced myself he would welcome the rescue animal once I described the dog and her desperate situation to him.

I prayed to God and had tremendous faith that He allowed me to discover a wonderful bulldog. I had high expectations for the potential adoption, but I didn't spend time pondering what God had to say about the situation. My selfish desires drowned out the persistent inkling that God was trying to communicate something to me. I crushed the doubts that crept into my mind. Due to my own arrogance, I thought I knew what was best and ignored all the troubling signs: nothing went right from the start. I should have ceased what I was doing and contemplated that this dog was not part of

God's plan for me. Instead of following promptings from God, I listened to my own voice.

In hindsight, I wish I heeded the apprehension I felt. It would have been wise to back out and run as fast as I could in the opposite direction. God tried stopping me in my obstinate tracks at the very beginning of this process. One evening when Wayne and I were spending time together, the phone rang. It was the rescue group's coordinator who wanted to speak to me about adopting Fiona. Although Wayne only heard my half of the conversation, he knew my responses indicated one thing—I had applied to adopt a dog and I was being questioned regarding my pet ownership experience, suitable home environment, etc. The expression on his face informed me of his tremendous displeasure. He had guessed correctly. After the phone call was over, I confessed what I had done and showed him the dog's profile on the rescue's website. He was irritated with my actions and begrudgingly agreed to see how it proceeded in order to appease me. I won a minor battle, but the victory was bittersweet.

Subsequent conversations with the foster family and the adoption coordinator led to frustration. I made it known that I had upcoming days off from work. I preferred adopting her at the beginning of that free week and a half because it would give us ample time to get acquainted with each other. I wanted to spend uninterrupted time with the new addition to my family before introducing her to my unusual work routine. I expected that my night shift schedule would cause additional stress. The dog would already be facing challenges while acclimating to an unfamiliar home. Adopting her sooner than later would facilitate a smoother adjustment period.

This was not meant to be. The rescue group was a stickler for its rules. I couldn't argue with them because I understood that regulations were necessary for the safety of the dog, and they provided consistency. No one wanted to see a rescue dog placed in the wrong home only to be mistreated again or returned because things didn't work out for the best. But there was no compromise whatsoever: I had to visit the dog at the foster family's home, which was over an hour drive each way from where I lived. Next, they had to bring the dog to my home to inspect it and see if it was suitable. I needed personal references. The vet clinic was closed on Saturday afternoons and Sundays, and I wasn't allowed to have the dog until they spoke with my veterinarian. Days, then more days passed. Every time the rescue organization needed a piece of information, there was a stumbling block. Someone was always slamming on the brakes and preventing me from obtaining this dog—I am positive it was God. The delays weren't coincidental—they were meant to send me a strong message. Each day was filled with frustration, and I began believing that maybe I wasn't meant to adopt Fiona. I should have carefully considered those feelings.

It seemed like an eternity before I received the news that I could have the dog as soon as I electronically paid the adoption fee. The adoption contract would then be sent to me, and I could arrange a pick-up time with the foster mother, Susan. Without delay, I paid the five-hundred-dollar fee via PayPal then sent an email to Susan and asked if I could pick up the dog the next day. Even though I no longer had my long stretch of days off to initially spend with Fiona, I still had two and a half days off from work. The foster mother agreed that I could get her on Tuesday, and I notified her I would be there around eleven o'clock in the morning. I would bring the signed contract with me when I received it the next day.

The anticipation of the adoption prevented me from sleeping that night. I was excited but filled with trepidation. Wayne remained silent. He met Fiona during the home visit because it was mandatory that we were both present, but he didn't share my enthusiasm about her. The dog was cautious in his presence and kept her distance from him. Susan and I were both tense when he walked through the doorway, but the overall encounter went well. I hoped he would grow to care for the dog. Every pet we owned together was a bulldog, but each of them was different from the other—they all had their own personalities. Without a doubt, Fiona would have a distinct personality.

The next morning when I opened my email and looked for the adoption contract, I was flabbergasted. The document was ten pages long. In excruciating detail, it outlined numerous regulations that we needed to follow after adopting the dog.

Upon reading it, I asked myself, "Whose dog is this going to be, theirs or mine? The rescue will have a hold on her and control my actions as a pet parent forever."

To name just a couple of examples, it noted which vaccines I was not allowed to have a veterinarian administer to her. They didn't care how good the vet was, there was no room for personal judgement. They also did not want any tick-preventative applied. I lived near a heavily wooded area that attracted deer and had found numerous ticks on my previous dogs. That mandate was absolutely ridiculous. In addition, they required notification if the dog ever became seriously ill and needed to be euthanized. One of my dogs had had extensive, incurable cancer that encircled her heart and invaded her lungs. Even in her dire situation, I would have had to ask permission to mercifully euthanizer her if I had rescued her through this organization. Their intrusive and over the top rules were beyond belief. I called the foster mother and voiced my concerns, stating that I didn't know if I could comply with and sign the contract. She convinced me we had come this far, and it was a shame to back out now. I wish I listened to my gut feelings that told me things were not right. It was probably God's voice of knowledge that was trying to warn me and tell me I shouldn't proceed with this adoption. I stifled any guidance from God—I forged ahead and drove to pick up the dog.

Fiona seemed excited to see me and scrambled onto the back seat of my car without assistance. She was eager to depart from her foster home. I allowed the foster family to spend a couple of minutes saying goodbye to her after we exchanged hugs. As Fiona's foster father leaned toward her and patted her on the head, he said a few words that I never forgot:

"Good luck, Fiona, you're going to a new home. I don't believe what anyone says about you; you're a good girl."

The words struck fear in my heart, and I had that terrible sinking feeling you get when you knew you completely made the wrong choice. As I drove away with the dog in my car, I wondered what other people had said about her. He gave me the impression that she wasn't such a nice dog in the past and there were things they knew or witnessed that I wasn't told. Later that day, I realized my suspicions were correct. It seemed like an unusually long ride back home, and the next two days felt even longer.

I was told it would take time for Fiona to adapt to her new surroundings, and she needed to be in a calm atmosphere. Considering I didn't have any children or other pets, my home was peaceful. Since I had experience with adopted dogs, I was well aware that there was an adjustment period for everyone involved. Some dogs needed more time and space than others. On the other hand, though, I wanted to show Fiona that I was her alpha guardian. Many dogs developed behavior problems when they lacked a confident leader and owner. I planned on setting simple but firm rules and would give Fiona some time to learn the boundaries while I demonstrated kindness and affection toward her. In theory, it was a good plan, but in practice, it failed.

During that first day, I caught her trying to dive into the kitchen trash bucket, and she attempted to tip it over. I could see her from the next room since my house had an open floor plan. Gently, I called her name and got her attention.

"Uh, uh, I see what you're doing over there. No."

I definitely had her attention because in the next instant, she came running at me from the kitchen. She proceeded to lunge at me with a wide-open mouth directed toward my face as I lounged on the sofa. Reacting swiftly, I put my arm up and blocked my face and body. I defended myself and pushed her back as she leapt at me several times. She managed to bite me once and then ceased the behavior. Shocked, I let Fiona retreat to a corner without saying anything else to her.

The following two full days did not get any better. She showed aggressive posturing toward Wayne whenever he entered the house even though she had initially been friendly toward him. She destroyed her blanket and toys when she tore them into shreds. The daytime with her wasn't entirely horrible, but as dusk approached, she acted like a completely different creature. She had a phobia of the dark and became a mean animal around that time, regardless of how calmly we behaved around her. The culmination was on Thursday night as we prepared for bedtime. Wayne went upstairs to bed a short time before me—the reality of a new dog in the home mentally exhausted him. I stayed up with Fiona for a little while longer then took her outside for a pee before attempting to settle her into her crate. She was obedient with her bathroom duty but, for an unknown reason, decided she was not going to spend time in the crate. As if possessed by demons, she started lunging at me again; she sunk her teeth into me several times. As a matter of fact, she bit me a total of eight times on both hands and arms. Somehow, I managed to get her into the crate for my own safety. She thrashed about and I backed away, fearing what she was going to do to me if I let her out. I left her alone and crept into the bedroom. I listened to what she was doing. It sounded like she eventually settled down without any intervention. My husband had already fallen asleep and was oblivious to what just happened. I was unable to sleep and stared into the darkness—it was one of the worst nights I could remember. I cried incessantly but muffled my sobs because I didn't want to wake Wayne.

I vividly recalled feeling anger toward God. *I asked you for a nice dog. I trusted that you would help me find a wonderful bulldog. What is this source of despair that you sent to me? Our lives are over; this is the most terrible dog we could have adopted.* I began blaming God, but something unusual happened: every warning sign that this adoption spelled trouble flashed through my mind. I reviewed all the promptings that told me this animal was not meant for us. I asked God how I could have ignored His messages and brought that animal into our home. Was I the one to blame?

God showed me that my intentions in wanting to rescue an animal were admirable but that I made a huge mistake: I didn't rely on what I sensed God was trying to tell me at the beginning of the adoption process. The frustrations I felt were the biggest clue. God fosters peace, not strife, and I should have listened to His voice in my heart. He gave me multiple opportunities to halt my actions.

Instead of patiently listening to and trusting God, I placed my faith in people. The rescue organization took advantage of the sympathy I felt for rescue dogs. They scrutinized my credentials and ability to care for a pet, but they were dishonest with me. They weren't forthcoming with the truth about Fiona. They should have shared all the knowledge they had about her. Instead, they held back details that would have allowed me to make an informed decision. I was sorrowful because I was deceived.

At that point, though, it didn't matter whose fault it was; I felt my life was over because I would be stuck with this vicious dog for the rest of her life. I didn't want a dog that I now hoped would suddenly drop dead from a terminal illness—I wanted a loving companion who would be a joy in my life. I was told she had been placed in a kill shelter and she would have died because no one wanted her and her owner was in jail. Guilt encompassed me when I thought that was where she belonged. She was a distressed dog who was probably tortured by her previous owner. I bet her prior living conditions were unbelievably inhumane. Dying would have put her out of her misery. Those thoughts made me weep even more—I loved animals and never wanted one put to death, but that was what I thought. I wasn't blaming the unfortunate dog; her behavior was the result of the abuse she endured. Her reactions to situations were ingrained in her as self-preservation mechanisms. She didn't comprehend that her behavior toward me was inappropriate.

The only solution I devised was calling the foster mother in the morning and telling her the dog was going to be returned to her. Wayne would never be able to take her to work with him; she was unpredictable and the liability was too high. I didn't know if I would ever feel comfortable having guests over to my house in the future. Susan was going to have to take the dog back because I was not going to give her a choice. Finally, I fell asleep.

That morning, I went downstairs and saw Fiona sitting on the sofa while my husband made coffee. She acted as though nothing unusual had happened, but I knew the truth. I feared for Wayne because I had to work that night and the next. It was essential that I warned him about her behavior, and I probably should have done that the night before. It was irresponsible to not inform him sooner of what she did to me; the same thing might happen to him. How could I live with myself if she ever mauled him? He deserved better, especially because I forced that dog into our lives. We simply couldn't keep her.

I prayed to God before I picked up the phone and called the foster mother. *Please let them take her back. She needs to go today. Please don't let me be stuck with her. Help me with a way out of this situation. I wanted it to work, but it's not right, and I now know this dog will never be the one for us. You tried warning me in a multitude of ways, but I didn't listen. I'm sorry. Please let me be free of her.*

Before I knew it, I found myself packing up Fiona's few possessions and driving her back to the foster family's home. The conversation between me and Susan wasn't amicable, but she agreed to take the dog back. She told me she warned me the dog didn't like men and that Fiona needed a calm household. I was never informed that this dog disliked men. I assured her there probably weren't many households that were more peaceful than mine. I was infuriated and resented how I was made to feel like a failure. Susan told me I hadn't given the dog enough time to adjust.

I asked her, "How many times do I allow Fiona to bite me before saying enough is enough? Ten bites in two and a half days weren't enough?"

I was certain she withheld crucial information from me that affected my decision to take the dog. In her desperation to get Fiona into a home, she glossed over Fiona's true nature and history. Susan needed to get her placed somewhere before colder weather arrived. The dog was living in an unheated, screened room that was attached to their house because she didn't get along well with their other dogs. I cannot prove my theories about the truth, but the foster father let some information slip out when I returned the dog—he mentioned she was aggressive toward their neighbor who once came over to visit. With a heavy heart, I dropped the dog off and started leaving. I looked back at her wrinkled face, and she tried following me to my car. If she could have been calm and sweet like that during the entire course of the day, I would have loved her. I was sympathetic to her dire situation, but I couldn't keep her.

I sobbed during the entire drive back home. It was Halloween. Trick or treat. The trick was on me. I adopted Fiona for less than a week, but the anguish of losing her was almost as intense as when Daisy died. I will never know what might have happened if we kept her. I was certain there would be no future dog for me; that experience tainted Wayne forever. It was a deed that could not be undone or forgotten. It wounded me to my core.

What added insult to injury was that I was told I would not get my five-hundred-dollar adoption fee back. That was another low-blow kick in the gut. I was informed that it was clearly stated on the adoption contract that the fee was nonrefundable. It took me a while to remember this fact, but I recalled being told I had to pay the fee first and then I would receive the contract. How could I have known the fee was unreturnable since I paid it before I saw the paperwork? I was tired and didn't want to fight about it. Part of me didn't care if I lost the money; I was grateful that Fiona was no longer a part of my life.

Fiona's foster parents were the ones who gave her that name. I renamed her Rosie for the brief duration she was with us. All of my previous dogs had flower names, and I wanted that girl to have one too.

Cheerfully, I told people who knew of the pending adoption, "Her life may have been terrible in the past, but her future will be rosy."

The name was appropriate but not for the reasons I imagined: that rose possessed sharp and painful thorns. I viewed the upcoming adoption and difficult obstacles I faced through rose-colored glasses instead of with clarity.

I was exhausted from the events of the day, but I was

less stressed out after I immersed myself in work that night. I thought about the adoption fee, the crushed hopes and dreams, and all the wasted time and effort over the past couple of weeks. I cast all those cares to God. He could get my money back for me if it was His will, regardless of what the contract said or however anyone lied; I wanted to put the entire issue behind me.

It wasn't a coincidence that the process of adopting Fiona was so difficult. God was communicating something to me. He gave me many reasons and opportunities to cancel the adoption before I proceeded with it. God didn't have to, but He gave me a miracle by removing that dog from my life after I prayed to Him. Within a couple days, He also returned my money to me—it was suddenly refunded to my PayPal account without any further struggles.

God was merciful despite my actions. He allowed me to make mistakes, and He also helped me through them. He resolved the bulldog fiasco without penalizing me. Instead, He continued loving and blessing me.

POPCORN

DURING A ROUTINE NIGHT AT WORK, AT two-thirty in the morning, my mind wandered back to my last place of employment and the people with whom I worked. When I worked in the hospital, the nurses tried to sit together at least once a shift. We'd eat dinner or share snacks. There was never a guaranteed slow time of night because a patient's condition could be unpredictable in an ICU, but activity was generally less hectic between two-thirty and four o'clock. A treat that we adored and ate was fresh popped popcorn. You could smell the microwave popcorn throughout the entire unit and it beckoned us to the breakroom. We always hoped that whoever was cooking the popcorn in the microwave was not distracted or walked away; an unattended and overcooked popcorn bag may start to burn. We didn't want to receive a visit from the local firefighters at that time of the morning after the smoke detectors alarmed. Shame on us if we caused a false fire alarm.

I reminisced about the buttery taste of that popcorn and the crunch of the kernels in my mouth. For a while many of us were addicted to kettle corn, which had a distinct sweet and salty flavor. Of course, there was the low-fat version that someone on a diet dared to provide as a healthy substitute. My mouth watered over the former of the two options, although almost no one refused any version of the snack.

In the first three years that I was employed in the e-ICU, I only had popcorn twice while at work. It just wasn't a tradition there, although we had plenty of other snacks at times. Everything from veggie trays to chips or homemade cookies could be found—but no popcorn. I longed to have some freshly popped popcorn and decided to add microwave popcorn to my grocery shopping list. All I needed was a small box of it, which I could bring to work to satisfy my cravings. I told the secretary and the nurses with whom I was working about my desire for popcorn, and we discussed our favorite brands and flavors. I didn't go shopping at the market that morning, though, because I was returning to work that night—I needed to go home and sleep. The popcorn purchase would have to wait until I went to the grocery store later that week.

When I went back to work that night, there was a nurse named Marnie who hadn't worked the night before—she had switched a weekend shift with someone. We were friends, and I was glad she was on duty that night. I wondered if Marnie wasn't feeling well or if she was having family issues because she was more quiet than usual. I figured I would have time to talk to her later in the night to see if she was okay. The start of our shift was a busy time because that was when we were setting up our workstations for the night. We needed to attend to issues that required our attention, and we started taking phone calls from nurses who requested our assistance. We'd have uninterrupted time to talk with each other later in the shift.

A couple of hours passed, and Marnie grabbed her car keys and headed toward the parking lot without saying a word. I knew she wouldn't abandon us—perhaps she needed to make a private phone call or was going to cry. As a courtesy, we monitored her patients and answered her phone calls while she was temporarily gone. We did that for each other, anyhow, such as when someone needed a break or an urgent run to the bathroom. No one knew why she left without warning; it wasn't any of my business, but she might volunteer that information to me at a later time.

She returned within five minutes. My back was turned to her, but I heard the magnetic click of the security door lock, which notified me of that fact. It wasn't until she walked into our break room area that I saw what she was holding: she had a *huge* bag of popcorn and began pouring portions of it into individual cups for us.

Who knew that a bag of popcorn could bring such joy? The popcorn was the rich yellow, buttery variety that reminded you of the kind you bought at movie theatres. No need to count calories, you knew that you would have to starve yourself for a week to make up for what you were about to consume. She set the cups down in front of each of us and told us to help ourselves to more. I thanked her for the popcorn and told her it was what I was craving. I had two witnesses—the secretary and the other nurse—who confirmed that was what I said the previous night.

As I nibbled on the tasty kernels, I contemplated whether the popcorn was a phenomenal coincidence. I was confident that it was God working through my friend. He knew what I wanted even if it wasn't a necessity. It was such a simple gesture that reminded me that God listened to me even when I wasn't praying for anything.

My friend told me that she and her husband took their youngest girl to the mall that afternoon. Both her husband and their daughter have a fondness for fresh popcorn. A vendor was selling popcorn, and they couldn't resist buying some. He packaged a large bag of it for them. Marnie placed the popcorn in the trunk of her car and forgot about it after they were done wandering in the mall. She used that vehicle to drive to work, and a few hours into her shift, she remembered that the massive bag of popcorn was still there.

"My family doesn't need to eat all that popcorn anyways. You guys can have it."

We gorged ourselves with popcorn, and there was plenty left over, which she took home with her at the end of the night.

Whether they are simple wishes, urgent needs, or longtime hopes and dreams, God knows how to fulfill them in His own timely way.

LITTLE GUY

NOVEMBER PROVED TO BE A DIFFICULT month for me that year. I was dejected because my life was void of a doggie companion. It would be the first time in nineteen years that I spent the holidays without a dog. Over the years, I had accumulated many bulldog-themed decorations and ornaments. I couldn't bear looking at them, especially the ones that contained photos of my previous dogs. I wasn't ready to see any reminders of those pets. I had no desire to decorate my house or a Christmas tree, which was a shame because that holiday only occurred once a year. I eventually convinced myself to accomplish the task of decorating, but it was done without enthusiasm. It reminded me of how someone felt when they lost a parent, child, friend, or other loved one during the holidays. I understood that kind of grief because people in my own life have died too. The loss of a pet was both similar and different. I trusted God to help me overcome my sadness. I gave myself time to mourn and kept my feelings to myself.

I didn't dare mention to anyone the idea of trying to find another dog through a different rescue group or shelter. Well-meaning people wanted to help, but it made me more depressed. Part of me was afraid to try again, and the other part of me knew it wasn't worth the tension it would cause if I mentioned it to Wayne. I looked toward the future and convinced myself that all things worked out for the best. I reminded myself of the freedom I had since I wasn't responsible for a dog that was going to be my new game plan. I stayed focused on the benefits of not having a dog, although I was frequently reminded of the advantages of owning one.

Sometimes at work when things were slow, I'd scan rescue sites for dogs. I didn't have any intention of submitting adoption applications and going against Wayne's wishes again. I'm not sure why I looked at those websites—it was an old habit that I hadn't broken yet. There were numerous homeless animals with adorable faces. They needed permanent homes, but many of those needs would go unanswered that Christmas. It saddened me when I thought of a dog spending Christmas alone in a shelter. Yes, I know— the dogs don't realize it is Christmas. They probably don't know the love and care of someone who wants them either. My heart ached for all the abandoned, unwanted, or mistreated animals of this world; they deserved better. The Bible states to look after orphans and windows in their distress. I'd like to think that God not only meant people but animals as well. I was satisfied with providing one dog at a time with a forever home, although I wished I could help them all. The only way I would be assisting any dog in the future would be through volunteering or financial donations. I'd rather open my home to one of them.

Thanksgiving came and went, and I knew that altering my pet circumstances was a hopeless situation. There was nothing I could do to remedy what went wrong in the past. I went back to the One who knows, and I prayed to God. In as simple a prayer as I could produce, I requested that if it was God's will, He would change Wayne's mind about pet adoption. I asked God once again to find the right dog for me because I still wanted one. God knows what we desire, but the Bible tells us we should pray for what we want. Examples of this are verses such as, "You have not because you ask not," and "Ask and keep on asking." I promised not to interfere and undertake an adoption on my own because I would mess things up again and make my home situation worse. Only God could bring a new doggie into my life. I knew in my heart that if an adoption situation presented itself to me, God would let me know if it was from Him. Then everything would work out for the best. Pray, have faith, and wait. That was what I did.

A few days later, in the first week of December, Wayne came home from work and was excited to tell me about a dog he met that day named George. George was a big bulldog, a male version of Daisy. My husband told me about this friendly dog who liked to play and was rolling on his back as Wayne rubbed his belly.

"Great. Sounds like fun. People can bring their pets into your shop, and you get to remember what it's like having a dog around. When will I ever get that opportunity?"

Wayne had no reply to my comments. We both knew I would hear about colleagues' dogs at work, but I would rarely have the occasion to play with one of them. I inquired more about the dog and learned that Wayne liked male dogs even though we had always owned females. We talked about other male dogs we knew over the years, including one who belonged to a former bulldog rescue volunteer we knew. There used to be an overweight male bulldog in the neighborhood where we previously lived. I told him I had never considered looking for a boy bulldog—I always wanted a girl even though we had a horrible experience in the past.

I stated, "There's a local boy who's up for adoption in Newport."

I didn't mean anything by the casual remark; the words slipped out of my mouth. It was as if I was thinking aloud to myself, and then I realized I said them to him. When I stated "local boy," Wayne knew I meant a bulldog and not just any breed of shelter dog.

Much to my surprise, Wayne responded, "Yeah, I saw him too. He seems nice."

I was astonished. Considering he never wanted another dog, what was he doing looking at rescue websites? I didn't ask. We briefly discussed the Newport dog since he wasn't resistant to the conversation. If he had told me to stop or repeated again "no more dogs," I would have dropped the subject, but he didn't halt the conversation. I asked if I could inquire about adopting that dog. We agreed that we would make it clear to the adoption agency that we needed full disclosure about the animal, including any known aggression, abuse, or signs of severe psychological illness. We were not going to get fooled again and didn't desire getting stuck with an animal who was misrepresented. Once bitten, twice shy, as they say. That night I applied for the dog named Bubba.

I knew that many rescue organizations were managed and staffed primarily by volunteers. They have jobs and families and may at times be overwhelmed by the amount of adoption inquiries they received. I didn't expect to hear from anyone anytime soon regarding the adoption application. When the phone rang the following evening, I was surprised I heard from one of the directors from the rescue group. She was amicable and I enjoyed speaking with her. I didn't mind her questions regarding my application or the type of home I thought I could provide for my potential new fur-baby. She seemed to answer my questions sincerely and was sympathetic toward my last adoption experience. It was heartwarming hearing her thank me for giving adoption another chance instead of becoming bitter and close-minded toward adoption as an option. Before I knew it, she gave me the name of the foster mother who was currently taking care of the doggie I wanted. I was told I'd hear from her soon. *Soon?*

It was more like lightning speed. Within the hour I received a phone call, this time from foster mom, Jenni. Similar to the conversation I had with the adoption coordinator, we both took turns and asked each other questions. We exchanged humorous anecdotes about our experiences with bulldogs. She wanted to come to my house with the dog so we could all meet. She would perform a brief home inspection for safety, which was part of the process of adoption. We decided upon a mutually agreeable time, and I promised to send her detailed driving instructions to my home via email. I was excited about meeting her and the dog the following week.

As expected, the next seven days progressed at a snail's pace, but it allowed me ample time to think and pray. I hoped for the best but expected the worst. I feared being disappointed and heartbroken again, but the situation was not the same as during the adoption of Fiona. Unlike the other experience where I encountered stumbling blocks with each forward step, Bubba's adoption flowed smoothly. The best way I could describe it was that there was a peaceful aura associated with it. I learned that if you followed peace in your heart, everything would be okay.

The day I was to meet Bubba the bulldog and Jenni arrived. With trepidation and joy, I greeted the foster family and the furry little guy they brought with them to my house. *Oh my, he really is a little guy.* Compared to Daisy, he was a compact young dog who was energetic and agile. He was curious, spirited, and friendly, which was a refreshing change from Fiona. Bubba was a handsome purebred with soft fur and well-mannered behavior. Off leash, he wandered around my home and was interested in his new surroundings. In the corner of the family room, a crate was set up with the door wide open, and toys were on the floor for him. He strolled in and out of the crate, then he pranced around with a toy in his mouth and wanted to play. The foster parents broke out in huge smiles and said it was a fun side of his personality they hadn't seen before. They watched as he chewed on one of the toys. He wasn't fond of their other dog, who showed dominance toward him and made him unhappy. That was one of the reasons they felt he would do better in a different home without other pets. It was obvious that they cared for him, but they wanted to find another home where he was content and could flourish during the remainder of his life. At one point, the dog rolled onto his back and welcomed belly rubs and gentle petting.

Jenni asked me, "What do you think? Do you want him?"

I looked up at her and chuckled. "Am I choosing him, or is he picking me?"

Simultaneously, and without hesitation, Jenni and her husband replied, "He's picking YOU!"

We all had a laugh together because we knew it was true.

Before I could say anything further, Jenni added, "He's free."

It was as if she read my mind, because I was about to ask how I needed to pay his adoption fee. Her comment confused me.

I parroted back to her, "Free?"

She understood my confused expression and explained further. They wanted him to go to an adequate and loving home. From prior experiences, the rescue organization learned not to post dogs for adoption without listing a required adoption donation. People see the word free and submit an application without fully considering the adoption consequences including future pet care expenses. The number of applications is further multiplied when the word free is associated with a purebred dog. Their way of eliminating the non-serious or inappropriate applications is to attach an adoption fee. Usually, if someone is willing to spend several hundred dollars on a rescue dog, they will take care of their investment. They probably have the financial resources to provide for the pet's future needs. This is never a guarantee, but it cuts down on the number of requests for the animal and eliminates those who want a cheap dog. Jenni didn't say if they eliminated the donation requirement in all circumstances; rescue organizations needed to obtain funding in order to care for the dogs until they found permanent homes. She knew I would have paid the amount that was listed on the rescue website.

I was astounded that the handsome purebred could be mine without an adoption fee. He was emotionally stable and already made himself at home in my house. Bubba was a fantastic dog.

"Yes, I'll take him!"

I stared at the bulldog. *God gives wonderful gifts without any strings attached. How could this precious, furry life not be a gift from God?* What Jenni said next confirmed that fact.

While I remained on the floor and played with Bubba, Jenni confessed something to me. She was surprised that she received a phone call so soon from the rescue director and was told that someone was interested in adopting him. She was informed that the potential adoptee—me—seemed promising because I had experience with bulldogs. I had no children or pets and owned my own home with a spacious yard. The rescue person relayed that it sounded as though I loved dogs and had a heart open to providing a "furever" home to a sweet doggie who needed one.

Jenni continued and mentioned the ironic timing of the director's phone call. That Sunday, she and her family attended church as usual. There was a prayer board in their church where anyone could post prayer requests and parishioners could pray for them. That church also had a traditional prayer group who met and gave special consideration to those specific prayer needs. Jenni told me she placed a card on the prayer board that asked people to pray for her foster dog Bubba. She desired that he would find a great home soon where someone loved and took care of him. The following day, she was notified that I was interested in adopting him.

I shared thoughts with her on my own experience. I acknowledged that the timing was, indeed, miraculous. While she and her local congregation prayed for Bubba, I was also praying. I told her I prayed that a terrific dog would find his or her way into my life. I didn't know how I would find them, so I asked that God would help the right dog locate me. I also asked God to re-open my husband's heart so he accepted trying adoption one more time; if anyone could make all that happen, it was God. And it was true—He did. See what happens when people pray together, or separately, for the same thing? The adoption was not coincidental—it occurred through the power of prayer. God united us for the same goal, regardless of whether or not we realized it at the time.

As we parted, Jenni's eyes glistened with tears as she hugged me goodbye. I reassured her that I would do my best to be an excellent pet parent. Whether it was the way they saw me interacting with Bubba or my story about praying for an unknown dog who became a part of my family, I felt they believed me. Bubba's family felt comfortable leaving him with me that day. I was thrilled that he remained with me, and I started getting him settled into his new home.

My husband came home that December night and was greeted by our newest family member. I watched the encounter, and all went well. Nowadays, it seemed that Bubba preferred Wayne's company to mine, but that was okay. I had the pleasure of having him all to myself while Wayne was at work. After nineteen years of dogs who bonded with me, I didn't mind that my husband had one who doted on him. Even though Wayne didn't want to admit it, he now had a dog who was overjoyed when he came home. Bubba was Papa's boy.

Isn't it astounding what happens when we wait for God's timing and go along with His plan, not ours? Bubba was my Christmas miracle that year, a living gift from God.

VIREO

THROUGHOUT MY LIFETIME, I HAVE BEEN A
nature lover. When I was younger, I dreamed of owning
a home with a spacious yard; I wanted flower and vegetable gardens within its perimeters. My desires came
true in the nineties after my husband and I bought a
piece of property in a rural area, and a home was built
on it. I planted trees and gardens in our new yard and
was content with the results.

I soon realized that no property was perfect or
immune to trouble. Over the years, I encountered
ravenous deer who ate my arborvitae shrubs and all the
buds off my azaleas and rhododendron bushes. Years
later, the rabbits stripped other shrubs clean. I cannot
forget the squirrels and chipmunks who dug up my

tulip and daffodil bulbs and left me without any of those flowers the following spring. It was the plight of the gardener, and I knew I was not alone in those universal struggles. I dealt with my gardening heartaches the best I could and utilized preventative measures, such as fencing, whenever possible. No animal was harmed.

Bugs were a different story. I desired a 100 percent organic garden, but out of desperation, I resorted to limited use of pesticides. A well was located on that property for drinking water, so I was cautious with the use of outdoor chemicals. I was also concerned about my beloved birds; it would have broken my heart if I poisoned any of those feathered creatures. Birds delighted me and made the property a special place.

Over years, infestations with gypsy moth or tent caterpillars plagued New England. They were notorious pests—probably worse than any other, in my opinion. I remembered those unsightly caterpillar webs in trees from when I was a child. Now, as an adult, I recalled the tree damage they accomplished in a single season—they were back in full force in Rhode Island. It looked like those pests were going to devastate all the trees that spring and summer. Everyone dreaded severe caterpillar infestations.

I valued the trees where I lived. They enabled me to have privacy in my yard. The trees were a natural barrier and provided homes and shelter for the birds. As I went for a walk down my street one sunny day, I was amazed that it sounded like rain within the woods, but it wasn't rain—it was the sound of those voracious, munching insects. It could also have been from the caterpillar excrement or broken leaves that fell to the ground. Regardless of what was causing that pseudo-sound of rain, there was no mistaking what I saw when I looked up toward the tree canopies: tattered leaves were everywhere. Many of the treetops were defoliated, and it was a deplorable site.

I did some research on the hungry pests that were eating the local oak trees, and the news wasn't encouraging. The prognosis for the trees was grim: it was predicted that the caterpillars would continue their diet of leaves for at least another full month. Considering the number of caterpillars that I saw *everywhere,* the massive army of them would win the battle against the helpless trees. I was disgusted by the sight of them on my trees, all over my house, in the grass, and on my driveway. No amount of pesticide spraying, short of aerial spraying, would control the infestation. I lived near the water reservoir for the state, so it was doubtful that aerial spraying would be suggested for that area.

A few days later, I went for another walk down my street and continued surveying the tree damage. More trees were affected. Double the number of shredded leaves were on the ground, and additional branches looked bare. The caterpillars weren't going to stop damaging the trees.

I don't know what made me think of this as I walked, but I considered the plight of the Mormons in Utah in the year 1848. I once read an account that stated locusts were causing devastation in the new Salt Lake City settlement. Crops were being destroyed by those notorious and ruthless insects, but the crops were saved by flocks of gulls who flew into the region and ate the locusts. I researched this story because it amazed me that the California gull (commonly called a seagull) was the official state bird of Utah. Living in a state with a lot of fishing and coastline, I couldn't fathom why anyone revered the gull and made it a state bird. Gulls, like pigeons, are sometimes considered pests because they leave trails of waste on anything and everything in their paths. The gulls on that particular occasion provided a valuable service to the Mormons.

As I continued walking, I used that solitary time to pray. Since the caterpillars were foremost on my mind, that's what I prayed about.

I know it is impossible to get rid of these defoliating insects by my own means, but God, you always have a way to solve life's problems. You are the one who led me to this scenic area, and you created all these trees. This is your land, and I hate seeing it destroyed in this manner, through insects. Please help me with this issue. Just like with the Mormons, please steer some bug-eating birds my way. Help them find my yard and rid it of the pests who are causing the damage. I love your birds and will help take care of them if I can. I will always welcome them into my yard. A few species of birds who were known to have a diet that consisted mostly of insects lived near my property. There were more than enough caterpillars though, which could feed additional hungry birds. *Please, God, bring more ravenous bug-eating birds to this area. I know you have the solution to my problem and requests. I cast my cares to you and will wait patiently for your answer. Amen.*

I tried learning to wait on God's timing because impatience was a problem for me. I repeated to myself "God's timing is not man's timing," but it was easier said than accepted. Often, we have to wait for what seems like an eternity before our prayers are answered. In this instance, God acted swiftly. God didn't waste His time when He decided to answer prayers.

A day later, I was sitting outside in one of my favorite chairs while I waited for my husband to join me. Relaxing together in the evening with our dog beside us was our summer routine. I decided to stretch my legs for a few moments, so I stood up and took a closer look at my vegetable and flower gardens. As I headed toward the back of the yard, movement in the trees caught my attention. I looked up and saw a bird that appeared to be picking at something on a branch before it flew away. The bird returned with something in its beak. I thought it was foraging for bugs, but then I realized it was building a nest. The crude nest was hanging from a fork in a branch. Not wanting to disturb the bird, I walked away and figured I could check it out with binoculars the next day.

The following day, I returned to that area and scanned the branches. What originally appeared to be a tangled mess of fibers was now a woven nest. I was excited that a bird was going to lay eggs and start a family in my yard, but I wasn't sure what type of bird built the nest. She was difficult to identify, but I determined that she was a red-eyed vireo. I spotted two of them hidden among the trees when I looked through my binoculars. I went inside and did more research on them. What I learned was exactly what I wanted to read—their summer diet consisted mostly of insects, and they were perpetual songbirds.

I didn't doubt that it was God who brought that pair of birds into my yard; it was a precious blessing. I was optimistic that the vireos and their offspring would satisfy their appetites with the caterpillars. To my knowledge, this species hadn't lived in the woods that surrounded my home in the past. God provided me with a new experience and birds I never saw before. He devised a plan for me with birds which were required for the caterpillar situation. I was thrilled the vireos graced me with their presence and arrived without delay. I'm grateful God sent them to me.

NEGATIVE
NINE DEGREES

COUNTLESS NUMBERS OF TIMES, I HAVE made plans to do something, and for one reason or another, those plans have been interrupted. I'm not alone in this issue—it happens to all of us. A parent, spouse, or child becomes sick, so we keep our priorities in order and stay home to take care of the person who is ill. At other times, our vehicle may have a problem, or another issue pops up. Regardless, it's usually something beyond our control that causes us to delay or alter what we want to do.

Our plans may not be completely disrupted—we simply have to make some minor adjustments and remain flexible. How we deal with these speedbumps in our itinerary is up to us, but I consider that a greater force is at hand. I believe God influences our plans and nudges us in the correct direction, altering events in our lives. Take, for instance, what happened to me on a bone-chilling day in January.

I had a few nights off from work and decided I wanted to go snowshoeing up in New Hampshire. I was inexperienced with winter hiking in the White Mountain area although I was familiar with hiking there during summer conditions. I chose what was supposed to be a reasonable hike for wintertime. I checked the weather forecast and trail reports and planned a hike up Mount Jackson. No snow was predicted for my scheduled hiking day, but I read that it was going to be bitterly cold. On the day of my hike, I woke up in the wee hours of the morning and armed myself with layers of appropriate clothing. I started my three-hour drive and expected to hit the trails before other hikers arrived. My goal was to complete the hike before sunset, which was at five o'clock—the amount of daylight hours was shorter during the winter months.

The drive up north was uneventful. It snowed the previous day, but the highways were plowed and didn't pose any overt danger to drivers. The New Hampshire Department of Transportation needed to be commended for how they cleared the roads and made the region accessible after snow storms.

My concern that morning wasn't snowy or slippery roads—it was the unavoidable cold weather. As I proceeded northward, I watched the outdoor temperature readings on the instrument panel of my car as they dropped. I hoped the temperature would level off at the freezing mark. Instead, it continued to lower until it reached a jaw dropping negative nine degrees.

Why didn't I stay in my warm bed? Who am I fooling? Is this hike going to be fun, or am I headed for a miserable day? I hope my new gloves keep my hands warm enough; I don't want to get frostbite on my fingers.

When I arrived at the area where I was supposed to begin my hike, the weather was the least of my worries. I pulled into a plowed lot next to the main road. When I looked around, I couldn't figure out where the hike began. According to my map, the trail started on the opposite side of the street, across from the parking lot. My problem was this: the plows which pushed snow off the roads also created enormous snowbanks. Snow, which was piled higher than six feet tall, obscured guardrails, street signs, and trail markers. How was I going to scale over those manmade mountains of snow? If I attempted crossing up and over the monstrous snowbank, I might sink into it, get stuck, or even break a leg. The mounds were close to the roadway and ate up a sizeable chunk of the breakdown lane. There was little room for error since tractor trailers and other vehicles sped on that secondary highway.

I was dismayed and frustrated; my hike up Mount Jackson was not meant to be. I was the only person in the small parking lot at that time of the morning, and I couldn't find and safely reach the trail across the street. After considerable thought, I decided to give up on that hike, but I didn't want to return home at that point.

A few times in the past, I made the effort to drive several hours to New Hampshire from Rhode Island but turned around and came back home without hiking. Once, it was because I was sick, but I didn't admit that fact to myself before I left home. I wasn't well enough to start or complete a hike that day. On another occasion, a trail parking area was crowded, and vehicles overflowed for miles onto the road. I didn't want to hike among hordes of people, and I didn't want to leave my car parked alongside a busy highway. At other times, trail conditions or weather were beyond my skill and comfort level, or forecasts and hiking reports weren't always accurate or up-to-date. During those times, I abandoned my adventure.

No, not today. I didn't drive all this way just to go back home—that would be a complete waste of my time, day off, and gasoline money.

I was determined to hike and had already formulated a secondary plan. Because of failed hikes in the past, I created an alternate itinerary just in case something went wrong with my first plan. I called my husband and notified him of my revised hiking agenda. My new plan consisted of a hike to Mount Waumbek, another mountain over four thousand feet in elevation. The start of the trail was a half-hour drive away, and it wasn't difficult locating it. I parked my car in a dirt lot at the top of a hill, and it wasn't long before I started climbing the mountain.

The frigid air made me wheeze, and I shivered beneath my clothes as I snowshoed up the trail. As the sun rose higher in the sky, my body began to warm up, and I focused on the splendor that surrounded me. The glow of dawn was replaced by a brilliant blue sky. Ice and snow clung to bare branches and evergreen trees and sparkled like diamonds in the sunlight. The hard packed trail crunched beneath my snowshoes and supported my weight.

If I had gone home, I would have missed all this. Thank you, God, for giving me the determination to hike today.

The motivation to hike that day wasn't the only thing that God gave me.

Shortly after I arrived at the sub-peak known as Mount Starr King, I was greeted by a tall, athletic hiker. His smile was as wide as the mountain range in the distance, and his cobalt eyes rivaled the hue of the sky. Up until that point, I hadn't seen any hikers, but it was inevitable that I would encounter other people.

Upon reaching the plateau where I was standing, he stated, "Wow, this is better than I imagined."

The magnificent vistas extended for miles, and we

both marveled at the winter wonderland in front of us. That anonymous hiker's joy, though, soon turned into disgust. He tried taking photos of the beauty with his phone's camera and noted its battery was dead. I understood his frustration; after you hiked for hours and reached a scenic peak, you desired a few tangible reminders of your efforts. It's natural to want to share a part of your experience with others. Photos also served as proof that you achieved your hiking goals. Sympathetic to his misfortunate phone issue, I offered to take photos of him with my own phone. He accepted my offer and posed in front of the snow-covered trees and mountains. I told him I would send him the photos the next day after I was back home. We exchanged phone numbers, which was something I never did with other hikers.

At that point, I expected he would continue with his solo hike, but he surprised me with a gift of appreciation. He retrieved a plastic bag full of loose granola out of his jacket and poured some into his hand. He demonstrated how a nearby gray jay bird would take it from his palm. I was thrilled as I witnessed this brief bird and human connection. Next, he took my phone from me and poured some granola into my hand, then took photos of me feeding the birds. This stranger, whose name was Bob, had no idea how much I loved birds. His gesture touched my heart that day.

Without saying a word, he motioned for me to join

him as we each still had a mile to hike in order to reach the peak of Mount Waumbek. Following behind him, I was amused as he chatted away and asked me questions. We had a few things in common, including our enjoyment of hiking and nature. He was amiable, and I felt calm and content in his presence. We reached the next mountaintop and took more photos. After that, we did not hike together back to our vehicles. He was a faster hiker than me, and he needed to return home before his child's school day ended. I assured him I would be fine hiking down the trail alone—that was my original plan.

I doubted that I would ever see or hear from Bob again after I sent the photos to him the next day. I learned that his family and his job kept him extremely busy. He wouldn't have the time or desire to keep in contact me. Miraculously, we continued correspondence via texts. His humor brightened my day, and I was excited to have someone with whom I could discuss hiking topics.

What I learned at a later time was that, similar to me, Mount Waumbek was not his planned destination for the day. I wanted to hike to the summit of Mount Jackson, and his itinerary included hiking up Mount Cabot. We each had to change our plans because neither of us could find where the trailhead was located. We both ended up on the Mount Starr King Trail and met each other in what you may call a strange twist of fate.

God intervened that day, and I believed I was meant

to encounter Bob, although I didn't know why. We never would have exchanged contact information if his phone had been working properly. We met on a Monday; he normally hiked during the weekends due to his work schedule while I preferred weekdays. Maybe I would benefit from having Bob in my life because of his sense of humor and hiking expertise. Perhaps he needed me because of my gift of encouragement. I might also be an example to him of what faith in God could do in a person's life.

People will come and go during different stages in our lives. God is able to alter circumstances and uses people as part of His plans for us. Bob and I didn't meet by chance.

MOOSE

"ARE YOU OKAY, MA'AM? ARE YOU HURT anywhere? Can you move everything?"

I was firing questions at the dazed elderly woman through the open passenger side window of her car. Adrenaline was pumping through my body as I tried to assess her, but I had to slow down and remain composed for her sake.

Despite a nursing career that spanned thirty-two years, I was never the first person at the scene of an auto accident. In the past, rescue personnel or plenty of bystanders were already present, so it wasn't necessary for me to stop and provide care. This was the first time I ever pulled my car over to the side of the road and inquired if my assistance was required.

I wasn't the initial person at the scene of the vehicle accident, which involved a car versus a moose in New Hampshire. Thankfully, I did not witness the gruesome accident. What I saw was a car with a crushed front end, and an enormous moose was dead in the middle of the road. I carefully navigated around the moose and parked in the breakdown lane of the road. I noticed that no one was beside the totaled car and its occupants. A few vehicles had already pulled over, and people were standing in the road, staring at the car.

I asked the woman nearest to me, "Are they okay?" as I pointed in the direction of the disabled vehicle.

She shrugged her shoulder, and someone else said, "I don't know."

Then what are you all gawking at? Standing here isn't helping them. Either do something or leave.

I ran over to the couple in the car as another man started doing the same thing. He proceeded toward the driver while I went and checked on the passenger.

Considering the condition of the car, I expected the passenger to have serious injuries. The front end was crumpled like a piece of paper, and the windshield was smashed and had a large hole where the rearview mirror used to be attached. *Did the hoof go through the windshield? Did the whole body of the moose bounce off the hood of the car?* I didn't want to imagine what happened. Female eastern moose average about six hundred pounds; that amount of weight caused extensive damage. At least the animal was not alive and suffering.

Thankfully, the passengers were not dead. The couple didn't even appear to be in critical condition; both were awake and talking. They were stunned but looked around and tried to grasp what had happened to them. The woman with whom I was talking started acknowledging my questions.

"I'm okay. No, I don't think I'm hurt." She demonstrated moving her arms and legs.

In order to keep her calm, I minimized the severity of the situation. I stated to her, "You were in a little car accident." I continued, saying, "I'm glad you're okay. Someone is calling for help, but I'm going to stay with you for a while. Is that your husband next to you?"

She nodded, and I kept chatting with her to keep her distracted from what was happening with her husband. The stranger who was at the driver's window had retrieved a first aid kit from his own vehicle and was assisting the man. *Thank goodness somebody's prepared for an emergency, because it's not me.* The helpful bystander was using gauze and picking pieces of broken glass out of the husband's forehead and hands. Even though the driver's skin was cut in those locations, the bleeding was minimal. I found his mangled eyeglasses in the car, and his wife was concerned that she lost her glasses too. I located the rearview mirror on the back seat of the car but didn't tell her that. I reassured the woman that her glasses would be found eventually, but she needed to sit back so she wouldn't scrape her forehead on the broken windshield. I felt useless doing nothing but talking to her, but maybe that was all she needed. It didn't look like she had any injuries at all—I had performed a brief assessment when I arrived at her side. A more comprehensive examination would be performed by EMTs. In the meantime, I didn't want her getting out of the car and passing out by the side of the road. I doubted that the vehicle was going to explode or catch fire after the impact. It was safer keeping her seated in the comfort of the car.

I couldn't comprehend the fact that the woman didn't outwardly appear to be injured. Her husband had scrapes from the broken glass but otherwise seemed uninjured. Then, in a single moment, the reason became clear to me. As I scanned the woman one more time, I saw something that I hadn't previously noticed. Around her neck was a chain with a cross pendant on it; Jesus protected her from harm. There could be no other explanation why neither occupant's legs weren't crushed when the car was wrecked. Other fractures or trauma to their faces should have been sustained. Her faith kept them both safe.

When the ambulance was approaching, I departed the scene and headed back to my own car. I walked past the moose again, and tremendous sadness filled my heart. Collisions between cars and animals unfortunately happen. I hoped that the cow didn't have a calf who would be motherless at that point; it would be a double tragedy.

During the three-hour drive home, I thought about the accident and how my day had transpired. I planned to hike a trail that I traveled in a circular route two years ago on the same day and month. This time, I only wanted to hike out and back to a scenic area, which would be a much shorter trip. That day, I didn't have enough confidence in myself to descend a difficult area of steep ledge. I aborted the hike at its halfway point and returned back to my car, disconcerted with myself. The hike was not a complete disappointment, though, because I found a serene spot along the trail near a waterfall. I ate my lunch in that location and contemplated the choices I made that day.

I believed that I was meant to be on Route 3 in New Hampshire at that specific time when I was driving home. Stopping for a lunch break may have kept me from being the one who collided with the moose. If I had hiked for a longer period of time, I wouldn't have been present to assist the passenger at the scene of the accident. I wouldn't have been a witness to the fact that a crucifix hanging from a necklace shielded her from injury. It was something I needed to observe for myself so I could share this story with others. Protection provided by God and Jesus exists. This was an obvious example that was graciously given to me for my book. How many times are we, or someone we love, saved from injury without realizing it?

A ROUGH ROAD TO
DEATH CANYON

WHILE IN THE MIDST OF THE COVID-19 PAN-
demic, I continued fantasizing about vacations and
hiking. By the end of 2020, restrictions were being
lifted, although airline travel was far from what was
considered typical. I had returned from what some
people might consider a risky adventure: I traveled to
the Southwest on a long flight and hiked in the Grand
Canyon. Like everyone else, I hoped that more restrictions would be eased, and life would return to the way
it was before the pandemic. I looked toward the future
and another autumn vacation the following year.

I decided that I wanted to return to Wyoming; it

became one of my new favorite places to visit, although I was fond of Arizona. I booked airline travel and lodging reservations. The next decisions to be made were where I was going to hike. Planning hikes was a pleasant distraction from household chores and duties at work. Looking forward to hiking brought a smile to my face.

I anticipated my next vacation, but during the winter months, I dreaded listening to news reports. Death tolls began rising as a resurgence of COVID-19 hit the United States and the world. People gathered indoors and celebrated the holidays—new cases of the disease began appearing each day. The nation wasn't free of COVID-19's death grip. The topic of death reminded me of a passage in the Bible. There are verses in the book of Psalms which mention walking in the valley of the shadow of death and fearing no evil. Those lines brought me comfort whenever life seemed grim because of so much death. I recalled stumbling upon that scripture the day my dog Daisy died.

It was ironic that I read about a region of Grand Teton National Park that was known as Death Canyon. It sounded both ominous and glorious. High above that canyon was a plateau area known as Death Canyon Shelf.

That's where I want to hike and camp. I want to walk through Death Canyon and live to tell others about it. I will not fear anything because God will be with me on that hike.

I obtained one of the coveted camping permits for Death Canyon Shelf. During the following months, I trained for the strenuous hike—carrying a backpack full of camping gear and a bear-resistant food container would be challenging. I prayed for hiking stamina, but I knew I had to physically do my part as well.

Months later, I arrived in Wyoming and was standing in the Jackson Hole Airport. Upon claiming my luggage, I walked to the rental vehicle counter, and an agent confirmed my reservation. He stated that there was a minor problem because there were no compact or midsize cars left on the lot—all that remained were sport utility vehicles. If I wanted a car, I would have to wait until one was returned, checked, and cleaned.

How can this be happening? I have a reservation. Doesn't that mean anything to these people?

The person behind the counter noticed the disgusted expression on my face. Before I had a chance to say anything, he notified me that taking the SUV as a rental would not increase the cost—I'd have extra legroom and baggage space without paying additional money. I decided not to wait for the small car I wanted to rent and agreed to use the SUV for the week. I signed the contract, took the keys off the counter, and was ready to start enjoying my vacation. I laughed when I saw the gigantic, gas-guzzling SUV—it was capable of holding eight passengers, but I was traveling solo. Unaccustomed to driving a vehicle of that size, I planned to carefully navigate the local roads and parking lots. Perhaps driving slower would cause me to see things I might not otherwise notice.

In retrospect, the SUV rental was a blessing in disguise. I had read that the access road for the Death Canyon hike was known as a rough road, but I could not find detailed descriptions of it. When the paved portion ended, the last mile was a narrow dirt road that was full of unavoidable ruts. A high clearance vehicle such as the one I was driving was the only safe way to reach the trailhead. Traversing that road in a compact car would have resulted in a stuck or damaged vehicle. The other alternative would have been to find a pullout area along the pavement where I could park and then walk to the start of the trail. This meant that I would have to hike an additional mile at both the start and end of the hike. I realize that to many people this doesn't sound like a lot, but when you're tired and carrying a backpack, every step matters. By the time I completed my two-day hike, I was grateful for the enormous SUV. It maneuvered over the road with ease and helped me omit extra hiking mileage.

God provided me with many mini miracles that were associated with that Death Canyon hike. Everything fell into place, and I was blessed with matters over which I had little or no control. I received a camping permit that allowed me to visit a magnificent area that few people in the United States experience for themselves. Along the hike, I spotted a moose cow with her young calf as they grazed beside the trail. Although the weather was frigid on top of Death Canyon Shelf after sunset, it was not raining or snowing. A full moon illuminated the landscape at night, and I scanned in awe the millions of stars in the sky. My feet never stumbled or slipped while I hiked. I was free from injury throughout the entire adventure. The SUV, which I thought was a curse, ended up being one of the biggest blessings. God knew how to work out everything for my benefit, and He transformed that rough road into a smooth journey.

CHAPEL—PART I

I WAS THANKFUL THAT I COMPLETED MY
Death Canyon hike on Saturday afternoon before the
skies opened up and torrential rain covered the region.
The rain, which continued into Sunday, became vari-
able and alternated between periods when it was light
or heavy. *What should I do today?* I contemplated my
options, which didn't include staying at the cabin all
day, even though a covered porch was attached to my
rental unit. I decided to head out and drove around
Grand Teton National Park. I brought hiking rain gear
with me in case I found a suitable area that I could
explore on foot during the storm. Sometimes it's relaxing flowing with wherever the day leads you instead of
following specific plans.

I entered the southern end of the park and saw a sign for a tourist site which I had not visited in the past. Usually, when I was in that region of the park, I was driving toward a hiking destination. At other times, I was fatigued at the end of a long hike and wanted to return directly to the cabin. Since I didn't have an itinerary for the day, I decided to check out a historic chapel.

The Chapel of the Transfiguration was an Episcopal chapel which was constructed in 1925. It was built so that the settlers of the region didn't have to make the tedious horseback or wagon ride to Jackson Hole each Sunday. It is a tiny building, but the mountains located near it are immense. What better place to construct a church than among all that magnificence?

As I approached the chapel, it dawned on me that it was Sunday. The church was more than a tourist destination—it had two scheduled morning services. I didn't want to interrupt the first one, which was in progress. I decided I'd drive up the road and then I'd return an hour later.

Although I am not an Episcopalian (I was raised as a Roman Catholic), I felt comfortable with the surroundings as I entered the quaint building. I embraced Christian beliefs and believed that all denominations should be able to harmoniously coexist with each other. I was a little embarrassed, though, because I was dressed more casually than I preferred when I attended church. I considered that God saw my heart and didn't care what I was wearing. I found an empty row of seats in the middle of the chapel and slid down the bench toward the wall. A large tour group sauntered in and out of the chapel before the service started. Otherwise, it was relatively empty except for a handful of people.

While I was waiting for the service to begin, I focused on the enormous picture window that was behind the altar. During a moment of relief from the rain, the Tetons, in all their grandeur, could be viewed. The site was impressive, and I marveled at how the altar and this window were strategically located. The glimpse of the mountains was short-lived as low grey clouds and rain once again overtook the area.

Even though the Tetons were obscured, I continued staring through that window. I couldn't see the mountains anymore, but I knew they were there. Isn't that the way it is with God? We can't see Him, but He is out there somewhere, hidden from sight. Especially during our personal storms of life, when things are murky, we want to see Him. We look for reassurance that He still exists and cares for us. Just because we can't see or touch Him, though, doesn't mean that He isn't with us and working in our lives.

Those thoughts were interrupted when the pastor started speaking. A few tears formed in my eyes, and I tried inconspicuously wiping them away as they started creeping down my cheeks. It seemed as though

God beckoned me into this chapel, and it touched my emotions.

At one point in the service, the pastor asked the attendees if anyone had a prayer request, regardless of whether it was for themselves or for someone else. He encouraged us to say the name or names out loud, and then we would pray for them as a group. I was a firm believer in the power of praying, including prayers of intercession for others. I welcomed the invitation and was one of the first people who responded. I stated the name of a friend who had suffered a traumatic brain injury earlier that year. I felt hopeful for his recovery if a group of believers worshipped together and requested God's help.

A few months later, I contacted that friend in order to wish him a Happy New Year. I also stated, "I hope this year is much better for you than last year."

He responded, "I'm sure it will be better—I can't imagine that it could possibly be any worse."

I inquired how he was feeling since we hadn't been in contact with each other lately. It had been months since I received an update on his condition. That spring, he told me he needed quiet time and space in order for his head to heal. Too much stimuli was not good for him. He was probably dealing with other issues as well.

That day, he sounded more like his usual self as he described challenges he still faced. His condition was close to normal. He acknowledged that he started feeling better at the beginning of October, and his health continued improving since that time. Unbelievably, he told me that he climbed Mount Washington in late December. During the winter season, he summited the highest peak east of the Mississippi River. His recovery from his brain injury was nothing short of a miracle.

I'm sure he gave himself all the credit for his recovery. He complied with whatever was necessary to improve his condition and provided himself with the best chance of living his usual life. I believed that prayer played a role in his health status. I didn't want to take credit for helping him become well, but I couldn't resist using that moment to share my beliefs with him. I hesitated before I sent the message—I was fearful of his reply because I knew he didn't embrace religion the way I did.

I told him, "Do you realize that I prayed for you every day after I learned about your traumatic brain injury? *Every. Single. Day.* When I visited a chapel in Wyoming, I said your name so that a group of us could pray for your health. I know you don't believe in those things, but I do. Regardless, you are well again, and that's what matters the most."

Joking in his usual manner, he responded, "I actually did some praying myself. But mostly, I was trying to figure out how to escape from the hospital." He thanked me for the prayers, and our conversation ended.

In the future, he may contemplate the magnitude of his brain injury and his miraculous recovery. I hope he remembers what I said to him and perceives the importance of prayers.

CHAPEL—PART II

WHO CAN COMPREHEND THE FACT THAT God sees and hears *everything*? Many of us don't conscientiously give much thought to how our behavior is viewed by God—we function on automatic pilot. We might be too overwhelmed to accomplish anything if we stopped and dissected every decision we made throughout a day.

While I sat in the Chapel of the Transfiguration, I thought about whether a financial donation may be asked of the service attendees. Collection boxes may have been located at the entrance to the chapel, but I didn't see them. I noticed two cowboy hats which were located on top of the piano but didn't realize they were utilized as collection vessels. In anticipation of such a request, I should have pulled cash out of my wallet and put it aside in a handy pocket, but I didn't. During the middle of the service, someone started walking toward me with one of the hats in his hand. I thought about retrieving cash from my bag when I remembered I had money in the back pocket of my hiking pants. I was reusing a pair of pants which I wore at the beginning of vacation because I never expected that I was going to end up in church. I didn't recall how much money was in the rear pocket; I retrieved it and peeled off the first bill which was on top and quickly placed it in the hat.

There was a time in my life when I may have thought, "I gave too much. I'm not working, and I could have used that money for something else." I was unemployed and my financial situation was tenuous. I was able to afford that Wyoming vacation because it was planned a year in advance, before I knew I was losing my job. I had pre-paid for the airline flight and rental car, and a fifty percent deposit was placed on my lodging. Common sense would have prompted me to cancel that vacation and seek refunds. I should have saved my money, but I wanted to go on that trip—it would be years before I could travel anywhere if I didn't obtain a reliable source of income. I expected that future vacations would remain at the bottom of my priority list.

As I sat in the chapel, I decided not to focus on negative or stingy thoughts. I wasn't going to waste my time with regrets about giving away the cash. God provided me with many wonderful things in life, including memorable vacations. He loves it when someone is grateful and cheerfully donates their resources to help others. Showing appreciation by giving back to the church and supporting it was the least I could do for Him.

The service ended, and I continued touring the area. I found a trail I could safely hike in the rain because it was neither steep nor rocky. It was still drizzling, so I encountered few hikers on that popular trail. I embraced the solitude and prayed as I hiked. The fog and mist reflected the autumn colors of the trees, and the area glowed with a surreal type of beauty.

My final stop for the day was a large hotel that contained shops and restaurants in its upstairs lobby. Having meandered through that hotel in the past, I knew I could find interesting Christmas gifts or souvenirs. I entered a crowded store that caught my eye. I noticed an employee who was assisting someone in the corner of the shop; that customer was examining multiple T-shirts. Behind me, a couple of employees were agreeing with each other as they spoke in hushed voices.

One of them whispered to their colleague, "That customer is going to make him go through every shirt hanging on the wall, but she probably won't end up buying anything at all."

They were correct; after wasting the employee's time, the woman walked out of the store empty handed.

Next, it was my turn. I decided to buy a pin that resembled a colorful feather, but I also wanted to purchase a grizzly bear T-shirt that was hanging on the wall. I approached the employee and asked if he could find it in a specific size. He located one, and I told him I'd buy it, along with the pin that I was holding in my hand. We walked to the cash register counter together, he looked over the shirt, then folded it and placed it in a shopping bag. He proceeded to scan the price of the pin—*twice*. I was curious because he made such an obvious error.

"Did you enter the cost of the pin twice?"

"Yes, I did." Without giving me a chance to say anything further, he added, "There was no price tag on the shirt. I'm selling it to you for the cost of the feather pin. You're actually getting it for a discount price. Don't tell anyone." He grinned as I paid for the merchandise and thanked him.

As I walked away, I was also smiling. It wasn't a coincidence that the amount of money I saved on the clothing was equivalent to the cash I donated in the chapel. Merchandise such as T-shirts were notoriously overpriced in tourist gift shops. Since I looked at other shirts that were sold in that store, I knew approximately how much money I was undercharged.

Earlier that day, I gave to God without grumbling, and He returned every cent of it to me. It wasn't as astounding of a miracle compared to my friend who regained his health. Nonetheless, I considered it a special reward from God who saw and devised everything.

NAPATREE POINT

I'M SURE THERE ARE MANY PEOPLE WHO believe that Christians who say they've heard a word from God are insane. It seems that hardly anyone believes you can receive a message from God. They don't understand that divine intercession doesn't have to be audible. Neither is it our own speech in our head. The voice of God may present itself to us as something we sense deep in our heart—it is comforting and provides us with peace. Believers also hear God speaking to them through words written in the Bible.

Once, on a sunny day in November, I had the privilege of receiving a nonverbal reminder from God. No, I wasn't in church at the time, and I wasn't at home reading my Bible either. I was strolling along a beach, admiring the ocean and local shorebirds.

Earlier that year, I decided to spend more time as a tourist in the state where I resided. I was ashamed to admit that I lived in Rhode Island for three decades, and there were many places in the Ocean State that I had never explored. In my free time, I stayed close to home or headed north to the mountains. When I planned vacations, my travels took me to states in the West or the Southwest; I wanted to view major national parks. I was ignoring the picturesque local coastline and the birds that occasionally called southern areas of Rhode Island home. I started making up for lost time and went birding during the off-season when traditional tourists were less abundant.

That was why I was in the Napatree area of Watch Hill in Westerly—I was bird watching. I easily found a parking spot since it was November, and I knew that the beach would be empty mid-week. The ospreys had left the area for the season, but there were still plenty of birds near the water or flying overhead. The waves were mesmerizing, and I sauntered along the shoreline, working my way toward the farthest end of that spit of land. Few people shared the beach with me that morning: a woman was playing with her dog, a photographer was observing the birds, and a young couple were walking hand-in-hand. I smiled and said hello to each of them but minded my own business.

As I proceeded toward the end-point area, I noticed something etched in the sand. In gigantic letters, someone had written, "JESUS LOVES YOU!!" I looked at it and grinned.

Yes, He does. Thank you for that reminder.

The phrase caused me to think of my friend Lisa. She would have been excited to see those words in an unexpected place. I should have taken a photo of it to show her.

Oh well, I'll just tell her about it when I get home.

The size of the letters on the flat beach would have prevented me from obtaining an adequate picture of it anyhow.

Upon returning home that afternoon, I sent a text to Lisa and told her about the Jesus message I saw written in the sand. I mentioned how I thought of her when I saw it, and I hoped she was having a good day. Lisa replied to my text and wrote something that surprised me. She told me my timing was impeccable and asked how I knew she needed to hear those words that day. She didn't disclose the reason, but she said she was having a rough morning and was extremely grateful for the message. I was thrilled that my text made a difference in her day. It would have been a shame if I overlooked that opportunity.

God spoke to me that day. Through a stranger's handwriting, He sent me a reminder. He also prompted me to forward those words to someone else who needed to read them. A timely message about Jesus isn't a coincidence.

LIFE PURPOSE

HOW MANY OF US, AT ONE POINT OR another, examine the direction our life is taking or the impact of choices we have made? People who are middle-aged may think about it the most. They don't know how many healthy or active years they have left and want to make changes before it is too late. No one, though, is immune from asking rhetorical questions regarding their life purpose. Without warning, we demand answers and may be dissatisfied until we figure it out. Nobody wants to waste their life or have regrets over past actions. Unfortunately, we can't see into the future—we can only examine things retrospectively.

A decade ago, there were several weeks when I considered future employment and life in general. I was going through a tough time at work and thought a lot about my life purpose. Work wasn't horrible or unbearable, but it gave me reasons to consider how my life was progressing. I was growing weary of the hour-long commute and felt tired due to a lack of sleep. Perhaps my body was rebelling after almost three decades of employment on the night shift. Interpersonal relationships at work also took a toll on me—a group of colleagues doesn't peacefully coexist 100 percent of the time. We sometimes worked short-staffed while new employees were being trained to replace the ones who resigned. Additional duties, such as expanded data collection, which required manual computer input, were tacked on to our workload. The cumulative effects of all of those things were making me unhappy. There was a night when I did a half-hearted search for other employment because of the dissatisfaction that kept creeping into my mind. I was determined, though, to stay where I was until God informed me that it was time to do something else with my life. I believed that God had given me that job, and it was my duty to stick with it. That employment was a gift when I had no other acceptable options. I showed up at work on my scheduled nights and performed the job to the best of my ability.

I considered the fact that I had *at least* fifteen more working years before I retired. I thanked God that I was able to work, which may sound strange to some people. I was grateful that I wasn't physically disabled or cognitively ill. I was also fortunate that I earned a college degree and was employed as a registered nurse. Regardless, I wondered if I would be working in a medical field during the next decade.

While cleaning my home on one of my days off, I stumbled upon a book on cultural literacy. It had been residing on my bookshelf for twenty years. I bought it when I contemplated going back to graduate school. It was one of a few prep guides I thought might be useful as I studied for graduate school entrance exams. An advanced degree would have allowed me to remain competitive with others if I pursued a job in management or as a professor. I gave it considerable thought and decided against going back to college—I knew it wasn't the right thing for me. I asked God what to do since I didn't know.

Is there a better way to spend my time? How should I be using my skills to assist people? Am I living up to my full potential? What truly is my life purpose?

The Bible says to ask God for wisdom and revelation. I was surprised by what God revealed to me.

We all have individual talent. I was gifted with the ability to encourage others and am also adequate in writing. Those are both things which I enjoy. God prompted me to combine the two and become an author. In my teenage years, I wanted to become a published author. I didn't think I had enough talent in that area and remained focused on becoming a nurse, but those writing dreams never died. God resurrected those dreams in His own miraculous timing. He provided me with phenomenal experiences and motivated me to write positive and inspirational books.

A few years after I began sporadically writing this book, I lost my e-ICU job. It was a telehealth job which was relocated to Texas. I was now unemployed because I refused to move away from New England. I viewed this major life change as both a loss and an opportunity. I lost a reliable source of income, but I gained ample free time that I could devote to creating books. Was this God's way of telling me that I needed to continue writing on a consistent basis? I now had the chance to focus on producing books without the burden of outside distractions and work commitments.

I was elated when my first book was published, although it was not this one. I didn't think it was a coincidence that I published my nursing memoir first. God knew there were tremendous amounts of things I needed to learn about writing, editing, and marketing. He didn't want me to rush this book into retail stores. God wanted me to carefully construct this memoir, and with His assistance, I made it better than its original version. The delay also allowed me to include several events that enhanced the book.

This book itself is a miracle because it was authored by someone who was a nurse, not a journalist, preacher, or English scholar. An unobtrusive and ordinary person became a published author. God uses the simple things of this world to confound the wise. People who seem to have no overt value by society's standards are used by God to fulfill His desires. He wants us to tell others about His grace, generosity, and wonderful deeds. I'm thankful that He used my voice and allowed me to describe circumstances which demonstrated His powerful love and perfect timing.

Through multiple experiences over the years, God showed me that mini miracles didn't occur randomly or through mere luck; He let me know they were from Him. These true stories are examples of how God bestows messages or blessings at the correct moment. Incredible things happened to me, and they can happen to all of you, as well.

Believe in God, not coincidence. Amen.

ACKNOWLEDGEMENTS

THANK YOU, WAYNE, FOR YOUR PATIENCE while I spent endless hours writing and marketing my memoirs. Becoming an author turned into a fulltime job—neither one of us was prepared for how our lives would change.

Karren, we met in college decades ago. Thanks for your continued friendship and words of encouragement. Sharing my triumphs with you means a great deal to me.

Chappy, you were one of my best cheerleaders when it came to my book writing endeavors. Your texts brought me immense joy and were appreciated. XOXOXO.

With trepidation I shared the first raw version of

my Christian manuscript with Lisa B. Her honest input and enthusiasm provided me with courage to continue this project.

Bob Finn shared his substantial marketing knowledge. Thank you for steering me in the correct direction and congratulating me when my efforts were successful.

Mike and Milena owned The Canyon Wren Cabins in Sedona when I visited that location. Thank you for your concerns for my safety when I hiked solo. You were both excellent hosts and a part of the wonderful memories I had in Arizona.

Thank you to Steve and Dawn Porter at Stillwater River publications for assisting me with the production of this book. Elisha Gillette created a cover which portrayed the simple design I requested. Tayler Greene contributed to the editing phase of this book.

Finally, thank you to the members of the Association of Rhode Island Authors who welcomed me into their group. I enjoyed meeting many of the authors at local events. It is a blessing to be part of an organization whose members support each other.

RAISED IN SOUTH DEER-field, Massachusetts, Ann pursued a career as a nurse and graduated from Fitchburg State College with a Bachelor of Science degree in nursing. She primarily worked in ICUs for thirty years. Showing dedication to her area of expertise, she earned both her adult critical care RN and cardiac surgery specialty certificates.

Seeking challenges outside of the workplace, Ann obtained her private and commercial pilot licenses in both single and multiengine airplanes.

Presently keeping her feet on the ground, she hikes and climbs mountains whenever possible. She conquered all forty-eight summits in the White Mountains of New Hampshire, which are above four thousand feet in elevation. Photography, birding, and cooking are her other favorite hobbies.

Her debut memoir, *When Being a Nurse Was Fun: Tales From My Life as a Nurse* was published in 2023. She wrote a short story titled "The Longest Journey."

It is included in *Rhode Trip*, an anthology produced by the Association of Rhode Island Authors in 2024.

Ann lives in Rhode Island with her husband, Wayne, and her rescue dog.

For more information, visit:
http://www.annwattauthor.com

If you enjoyed this book, please consider posting a rating or review wherever it was purchased or on a book reading website. Positive ratings from readers like you help others who are making book buying decisions. Thank you in advance for your assistance.